LIVING A LIFE THAT MATTERS

SANFORD ZENSEN

LIVING A LIFE THAT MATTERS

HOW TO REVOLUTIONIZE YOUR PERSONAL AND SPIRITUAL LIFE

WIPF & STOCK · Eugene, Oregon

LIVING A LIFE THAT MATTERS
How to Revolutionize Your Personal and Spiritual Life

Copyright © 2025 Sanford Zensen. All rights reserved. Except for brief quotations in critical publications or reviews, no part of this book may be reproduced in any manner without prior written permission from the publisher. Write: Permissions, Wipf and Stock Publishers, 199 W. 8th Ave., Suite 3, Eugene, OR 97401.

Wipf & Stock
An Imprint of Wipf and Stock Publishers
199 W. 8th Ave., Suite 3
Eugene, OR 97401

www.wipfandstock.com

PAPERBACK ISBN: 979-8-3852-3774-6
HARDCOVER ISBN: 979-8-3852-3775-3
EBOOK ISBN: 979-8-3852-3776-0

Unless otherwise noted Scripture quotations are taken from the *New American Standard Bible®* (NASB), Copyright © 1960, 1962, 1963, 1968, 1971, 1972, 1973,1975, 1977, 1995 by The Lockman Foundation. Used by permission. www.Lockman.org.

Scripture quotations marked (ASV are taken from the *American Standard Version* (1901), Public Domain.

Scripture quotations marked (AMP) are taken from the *Amplified® Bible*, Copyright © 2015 by The Lockman Foundation. Used by permission. www.Lockman.org.

Scripture quotations marked (AMPC) are taken from the *Amplified Bible, Classic Education,* Copyright © 1965 2015 by The Lockman Foundation. Used by permission. www.Lockman.org.

Scripture quotations marked (ESV) are from *The Holy Bible, English Standard Version®* (ESV®), copyright © 2001 by Crossway, a publishing ministry of Good News Publishers. Used by permission. All rights reserved.

Scriptures marked (KJV) are taken from the *King James Version*, public domain.

Scripture quotations marked (MSG) are taken from *The Message*, copyright © 1993, 1994, 1995, 1996, 2000, 2001, 2002 by Eugene H. Peterson. Used by permission of NavPress. All rights reserved. Represented by Tyndale House Publishers, Inc.

Scripture marked (NKJV) taken from the *New King James Version*®. Copyright © 1982 by Thomas Nelson. Used by permission.

Scripture quotations marked (NIV) are taken from the Holy Bible, *New International Version*®, NIV®. Copyright © 1973, 1978, 1984, 2011 by Biblica, Inc.™ Used by permission of Zondervan. All rights reserved worldwide. www.zondervan.com The "NIV" and "New International Version" are trademarks registered in the United States Patent and Trademark Office by Biblica, Inc.™

Scripture quotations marked (NLT) are taken from the Holy Bible, *New Living Translation* Copyright © 1996, 2004, 2007 by Tyndale House Foundation. Used by permission of Tyndale House Publishers Inc., Carol Stream, IL 60188. All rights reserved. New Living, NLT, and the New Living Translation logo are registered trademarks of Tyndale House Publishers.

Scripture quotations marked (PHILLIPS) are taken from *The New Testament in Modern English*, copyright 1958, 1959, 1960 J.B. Phillips and 1947, 1952, 1955, 1957, 1976, The MacMillan Company, New York. Used by permission. All rights reserved.

Scripture quotations marked (TPT) are from *The Passion Translation*®. Copyright © 2017, 2018 by Passion & Fire Ministries, Inc. Used by permission. All rights reserved. ThePassionTranslation.com.

Scripture quotations marked (ASV) are taken from *American Standard Version*, Public domain.

Bracketed [ ] comments in Scripture and quotes are the author's.

"But woe unto those weak and timid souls who are divided between God and their world! They want, and they do not want. They are torn by passion and remorse at the same time. They fear the judgments of God and of others. They have a horror of evil and a shame of good. They have the pains of virtue without tasting its sweet consolations. O, how wretched they are!" [1]
— **François Fénelon (1651-1715),**
a French Archbishop

It matters how we live.
It matters how we practice life…

---

[1] Richard J. Foster and James Bryan Smith, *Devotional Classics*, (New York, NY: Harper Collins, 1993), 48.

CONTENTS

Contents v
Introduction 1
Chapter 1 .... **15**
   The Authentic Christian Life 15
Chapter 2 .... **28**
   Live Under the Authority of God 28
Chapter 3 .... **41**
   Walk Daily in the Light of God's Word 41
Chapter 4 .... **63**
   Engage the World 63
Chapter 5 .... **77**
   "We Can Do It If We Will"—The Purpose and Plan of God 77
Chapter 6 .... **89**
   Live in the Presence of God 89
Chapter 7 .... **107**
   Make a Personal, Intimate Relationship with God 107
Chapter 8 .... **126**
   Glorify God in Attitude and Action 126
Chapter 9 .... **143**
   Talk with God…A Lot 143
   Conclusion 156
   Other Books by Sanford Zensen 162
   About the Author 163

"You can't go back and make a new start, but you can start right now and make a brand new ending."[2]
— **James R. Sherman, Rejection**

---

[2] James R. Sherman, *Rejection,* (Golden Valley, Minnesota: Pathway Books, 1982), 45.

INTRODUCTION
IT MATTERS HOW WE DO LIFE

John Stonestreet, president of the Colson Center, observed:

Young people (including older adults) don't need another institution to make them feel good. They need one that will tell them the truth about sin and the Savior who calls them to be transformed in the world, not conformed to it.[3]

Billy Sunday put it like this. "The churches don't need new members half as much as they need the old bunch made over."[4] That stings. He's talking about me. I count myself among the spiritually immature who need to grow up in the faith and represent the name of Christ and His kingdom better than I have. Improvements are certainly necessary. D.L. Moody indicated that "he would rather wake up a slumbering church than a slumbering world."[5] Somebody wake me up, please!

The importance of living an unencumbered, significant, purposeful, genuine Christian life and living like it matters, especially in the current secular age—cannot be overstated. We should never be satisfied with immaturity and a less-than-stellar spiritual life experience. We can be better, and we must do better if

---

[3] John Stonestreet, The Point: A Failed Formula, Breakpoint Colson Center, May 3 2017, Retrieved from https://breakpoint.org/a-failed-formula/.
[4] Editors, Echoes from Glory: Billy Sunday Sayings, Wholesome Words.org, 1996-2022. Retrieved from https://www.wholesomewords.org/echoes/sundaysays.html.
[5] William R. Moody, The Life of Dwight L. Moody by His Son, (New York, New York: Fleming H. Revell Company, 1900), 229.

we are to positively impact this world more than we have in the past. I must do better. I know this may come as a surprise to some, even eye-opening for others—I'm not perfect. I have yet to arrive as the consummate Christian, the complete spiritual package, the paragon of Christlikeness.

I've fallen way short of God's standard more times than I care to admit. In fact, I've often felt much like Charlie Brown, who complained, "Sometimes I lie awake at night, and I ask, 'Where have I gone wrong?' Then a voice says to me, 'This is going to take more than one night."[6]." Sounds much like my Christian experience. C.S. Lewis reminded us in his classic, *Mere Christianity,* that Jesus warned people to "count the cost" before becoming Christians.

'Make no mistake,' (God says), 'if you let Me, I will make you perfect. The moment you put yourself in My hands, that is what you are in for. Nothing less, or other, than that. You have free will, and if you choose, you can push Me away. But if you do not push Me away, understand I am going to see this job through…'

"The job," Lewis insists, "will not be completed in this life: but He (God) means to get us as far as possible before death. That is why we must not be surprised if we are in for a rough time."[7] I can personally attest to that fact.

The Apostle Paul *"urged"* (begged, exhorted, appealed to) the assembly of believers in Rome, who were trying to live successfully in a pagan, self-reliant world:

---

[6] Charles Shultz, Quote found in Psychology of Men, Word Press, Fall 2008. Retrieved from https://psychofmen.wordpress.com/interesting-quotes-by-famous-men/charlie-brown/.
[7] C.S. Lewis, Mere Christianity, (Hammersmith, London: HarperCollins, 1942), 202-204.

> Romans 12:2, (PHILLIPS) - *Don't let the world around you squeeze you into its own* mould (rather, be God's man, about God's business, in God's kingdom]. *Be holy* (in everything you do, unique, different, exceptional, like Jesus)...*let God re-mould your minds from within,* (so you can see life from His perspective), *so that you may prove in practice that the plan of God for you is good, meets all his demands and moves* (you and me) *towards the goal of true maturity.*

To the church in Ephesus and the surrounding area, Paul begged Christians "...*to live a life worthy of the calling to which you have been called [that is, to live a life that exhibits godly character, moral courage, personal integrity, and mature behavior]*" (Ephesians 4:1, AMPC).

In short, live a life that matters.

Genuine Christianity is life with substance, with depth, with certainty, and with a focus on the essentials: *"faith, hope, and love"* (cf. 1 Corinthians 13:13). *"Let your light shine before* [in the sight of] *others, so that they may see your good works and give glory* (more on that later) *to your Father who is in heaven"* (Matthew 5:16, ESV). These are the words Jesus used to describe the aim and goal of daily living—a life lived to the glory of God.

It matters how you and I live. It matters whether we are accurately reflecting and promoting the values and life priorities of Jesus, His Word, and His worldview. Adhering to biblical standards will build a quality life. Popular opinion can't do it, and neither will the vain and empty *philosophies* of this current culture (Colossians 2:8) with its questionable moral and ethical behavior, and purposeless living.

Anthony Hopkins, who won the Oscar for Best Actor in 2021, was asked in an interview about being happy and satisfied with his life. He was eighty-three years old at the time when he reflected back over his career and his life. He said,

> The irredeemable past—we can never go back (He's right on that point). The sadness of life is that we go on—we're born in this world, and at the end, we leave, and you think, 'What was that all about?' My life... at the end of it all, I don't know... what's it all about? Is there meaning in it? So what makes me really happy is—what makes me free—is the feeling that nothing is of that much importance. We're pretty insignificant little dots in our vast universe... Who cares, finally, in the end? I know nothing. I'm insignificant. It's all meaningless to me... (So) Enjoy it while it lasts.[8]

A rather dismal, shortsighted description of life without purpose or meaning. I need a better perspective to get out of bed each morning, to make the most of the day and the opportunities it may bring. I want to live like it matters. My life need not be "meaningless," for I am (as you are) more than a little dot in a "vast universe." I am a human being made in the image of God, a son of the Most High, clothed in the righteousness of Christ my Savior, and a man with value and great worth, who has found his place in this world—a place of significance—living out the plan and purpose of God for his life. A life that matters in God's big universe. I'd rather live a life that matters to God than follow the world into the abyss. Life can be a living hell.

---

[8] Chris Heath, "Anthony Hopkins Expects Nothing and Accepts Everything," *GQ,* (4-27-21).

I'd rather have Christ and Christianity as my guide, and the Bible as my guidebook for daily living. "I'd rather have Jesus… I'd rather be led by His nail-pierced hand."[9] Nothing else will do.

Phil Robertson (of Duck Dynasty fame) got it. Following years of reckless living, getting high and drunk, and ruining his life, Robertson determined that:

> Politics won't save you. Science can't give you the power to sidestep death. The pleasures and joys of this world are fleeting at best, damaging counterfeits at worst. But I have good news for you: Jesus offers life, joy, and peace…[10]

A new perspective. A new direction in life. A new sense of hope and satisfaction with daily living. Author and poet A.E. Housman (1859–1913) wrote *The Isle of Portland* following the close of World War I. It was a bleak, pessimistic assessment of life as he saw and experienced it.

Death claimed the life of a close friend, who may have hung himself. The tragedy of suicide runs deep and wide, leaving Housman in utter despair, hopeless, and struggling to make sense of his loss. Nothing seemed to matter anymore. The war had taken its toll, and man's greatest enemy had raised its head once again. Housman lamented to his friends, "In all the endless road you tread, there's nothing but the night…[11] For Housman, life had become little more than a senseless, pointless existence, with no clear direction or destination other than the grave.

---

[9] Rhea F. Miller, *I'd Rather Have Jesus*, Public Domain, 1922.
[10] Phil Robertson, *I Could Be Wrong But I Doubt It*, (Nashville, Tennessee: Nelson Books, 2024), Face Book post, July 2, 2024.
[11] A.E. Housman, *The Shropshire Lad*, (Project Gutenberg eBooks public domain, 1896), XVI, LX.

I don't want that. We can be and do better. "The mystery of human existence," said Fyodor Dostoevsky, "lies not in just staying alive, but in finding something to live for."[12]

The writer of the Epistle to the Hebrews told his readers to *"Keep your eyes on Jesus* [that's key]*, who both began and finished this race we're in. Study how he did it. Because he never lost sight of where he was headed—that exhilarating finish in and with God* (Hebrews 12:1-3, MSG). Paul summarized the entire Christian life: *"Watch what God does, and then you do it"* (Ephesians 5:1, MSG), loving people, living biblically, and proclaiming clearly and precisely the Gospel of redemption in Jesus Christ. It's the "good news" that matters, and the world needs to hear and see it in me. I need it, too, and it is what makes life worth living.

I know a recently retired Christian man (in his 70s) who slept in his backyard hammock during the coldest of winter nights to prepare for an upcoming camping trip into the Smoky Mountains with his grandsons. He was going to be ready, determined, and dedicated to his cause. His wife revealed her husband's life motto, which he had adopted, believed, and lived. Here it is:

> Life is not a journey to the grave with the intention of arriving safely in one pretty and well-preserved piece, but to slide across the finish line broadside, thoroughly used up, worn out, leaking oil, and shouting GERONIMO!!![13] - *Anonymous.*

I love it. The man has been described as "unique, eccentric, and crazy." He is certainly all of that and more. But somewhere through

---

[12] Fyodor Dostoevsky, *The Brothers Karamazov*, Translated by Andrew H. MacAndrew, 1970 (New York, New York: Bantam Books, Book V: Pro and Contra, Chapter 5: The Grand Inquisitor), 306-307.
[13] Becky Harrison, Life motto, *Facebook*, January 15, 2024

the years, he had learned how to make life count—not to whittle away the day or his future, but to live like it matters, going beyond the mundane and the ordinary, holding nothing back, and taking full advantage of every opportunity presented to him. A wise man who chose life—who built his life, if you will, Geronimo style—and made it count now, today, and for all eternity. He is a believer. It matters how we practice life. I'll rest when my feet hit the grave.

Paul spoke candidly to Christians.

> **Ephesians 4:1, MSG** - *I want you to get out there and walk—better yet, run!—on the road God called you to travel. I don't want any of you sitting around on your hands. I don't want anyone strolling off, down some path that goes nowhere.*

How you and I choose to live matters. Following in the footsteps of Christ matters. Emulating Him in *"word and deed,"* believing as He believed, teaching what He taught, doing what He did, forgiving as He forgave, and submitting to the will and authority of God the Father as He did—all of it, every bit of it and more, matters. How the world sees me matters, because in me, my friends and family may just catch a glimpse of Jesus (Galatians 2:20). Speaking as He spoke, loving as He loved, and giving as He gave—unselfishly, graciously, and mercifully—so that others might also be free to live life well, all to the glory of God the Father, matters. It all matters every minute of every day. What's important to God in Christ is important (or at least it should be) to His followers, and it should be important to you and me. In the end, it is the only thing that truly matters.

Moses stood before the people for his final address. He was now an old man, looking in the rearview mirror, seeing his life over the last one hundred and twenty years—from his boat ride down the Nile in a wicker basket to standing on the brink of the Jordan and the promised land. He had seen much but learned more. His wandering in the wilderness with a rebellious, obstinate, unreliable bunch of yahoos (that's Hebrew for "boneheads") taught him a great deal about life.

His words are a prescription for living life like it matters and wringing the very best out of every day.

Read it carefully.

> **Deuteronomy 30:15-19, NIV** — *See, I set before you today life and prosperity,* (one or the other) *death and destruction.* (Take your pick). *For I command you today* (if you want life) *to love the Lord your God, to walk in obedience to him, and to keep his commands, decrees and laws; then* (conditional) *you will live and increase, and the Lord your God will bless you in the land you are entering to possess.* (So far, so good, but read on). *But* (here comes the tough part) *if your heart turns away and you are not obedient, and if you are drawn away to bow down to other gods* (gods can come in a variety of forms) *and worship them, I declare to you this day that you will certainly be destroyed. You will not live long in the land you are crossing the Jordan to enter and possess...*
>
> *Now choose life* (the smart choice), *so that you and your children may live and that you may love the Lord your God, listen to his voice, and hold fast to him. For the Lord is your life...*

Love, Listen. Hold fast. Not much else needs to be said—God's life-giving principles for living a life that matters.

The senior pastor of Harvest Christian Fellowship in Riverside, California, Greg Laurie, posted a recent video of singer Michael Bublé sharing his thoughts on what real life is about. This is from a man with global recognition who has reached the heights of the recording industry (seventy-five million records sold). Here is what he said about what successful living looks like:

> Rich isn't what you think it is. That word "rich" your friends use, sounds like money and stuff and Lamborghinis, and tickets to go see Messi (the Argentine national soccer star). That's not rich. Rich is having a strong faith. Rich is having a great family and loving your family. Rich is having great friendships…(not) the money. The people I know that have the most stuff are the most miserable people I know. And I don't know how else to explain it, you know…Somebody watching this podcast might say, 'That's easy for you to say, Bublé, you got a lot of stuff." It doesn't take long to realize that life has nothing to do with stuff. We're all sitting on our death bed. We are all going to die, every one of us, and nobody looks back and says, "I wish I collected more stuff."[14]

God has a better plan for my life, and I want in on it—living a life that matters.

John the Apostle revealed in his Gospel the foundation upon which Jesus built a life that made a difference—a difference that changed the world and eternity. Let it be said—I want to live like Him—passionately, intentionally, and productively. A life with divine purpose, direction, understanding, and courage; enabled and

---

[14] Greg Laurie, Statements from Michael Bublé (video), Facebook Post, July 25, 2024.

empowered, supernaturally equipped to get this thing called life done, and to do it day in and day out with all the gusto I can muster. American psychologist Abraham Maslow believed, "If you deliberately plan on being less than you are capable of being, then I warn you that you'll be unhappy for the rest of your life."[15] I'll skip the unhappy part, and plan to get in on God's best for my life.

You and I are made for so much more, more than we might imagine. We are "capable of being" all that God has intended for us to be and do. Take heart, old people. Caleb was eighty years old with the strength of a young man, demanding of Joshua, *"Give me this mountain...with great fortified cities...and I shall drive them (the Anakim) out"* (Joshua 14:12). A man with the heart of a lion, a man made *"for war and for going out and coming in"* (Joshua 14:11). Life was not going to pass him by. Not a chance. That was not going to happen. He would follow God, as he always had, to the ends of the earth. Not my will, but God's from start to finish. I want every waking moment to count, and so did Caleb. Life is too short to settle for anything less.

This book is a call back to the basics, to a simpler faith and a bibliocentric approach to daily living. What follows in the chapters ahead are some of the statements Jesus made of Himself and a record of His actions during His life and ministry, as recorded by the Apostle John. Collectively, every principle listed (not an exhaustive list by any means) made Jesus' life a success in fulfilling all that God the Father had for Him. His record can be your record and mine, with the same redemptive results. For those who dare answer the divine call to *"Follow Me"* (Christ) and imitate God in love and sacrifice (Ephesians 5:1), a truly meaningful life is made possible

---

[15] Nathan Davidson, 50 best psychology quotes: A list of psychological deep quotes about life, Thriveworks, retrieved from https://thriveworks.com/blog/greatest-psychology-quotes-ever/.

and within reach of us all. Paul ordered believers at Ephesus, *"You be imitators of God."* That's pretty straightforward.

At seventy-six years old, one of the most influential women of her generation, Eleanor Roosevelt, published *You Learn by Living: Eleven Keys for a More Fulfilling Life*. She put to paper the principles that worked in her personal and public life. She had learned how to make the most of her days. In that book, *s*he commented:

> Mozart (1756–1791), who was buried in a pauper's grave, was one of the greatest successes we know of, a man who in his early thirties had poured out his inexhaustible gift of music, leaving the world richer because he had passed that way. To leave the world richer—that is the ultimate success.[16]

I think she was on to something. Jesus successfully managed His daily affairs and ministry, and left the world a much richer place. He left us an example to follow. As you read the record of His incredible, world-changing life, you will discover the means and methods He employed to live a life of significance and meaning—a richness beyond measure.

Here are nine principles for daily living. They are important, all of them. There is nothing new here, but they do matter, each one in their own right, without exception. Collectively, they become the secret to revolutionizing and energizing your personal and spiritual life. In fact, there is nothing secretive about any of them—just a foundational approach to living a life that gets the best results.

---

[16] Elenor Roosevelt, *You Learn by Living: Eleven Keys for a More Fulfilling Life*, (Louisville, Kentucky: Westminster John Knox Press, 1960), 119.

1. BE AUTHENTIC – A MASTERPIECE IN THE MAKING (John 3:16; John 4:26).
2. ANCHOR YOUR LIFE TO THE AUTHORITY OF GOD (John 8:42, 12:49-50).
3. WALK DAILY IN THE LIGHT OF GOD'S WORD (John 8:12, 31-32; 17:17).
4. ENGAGE YOUR CULTURE AND GENERATION WITH THE TRUTH OF THE GOSPEL AND THE WORKS OF CHRIST (John 4:5-10).
5. "WE CAN DO IT IF WE WILL" - THE PLAN AND PURPOSE OF GOD (John 4:34; 5:30).
6. LIVE DAILY IN THE PRESENCE OF GOD (John 8:29; 16:3).
7. MAKE A PERSONAL, INTIMATE RELATIONSHIP WITH GOD, THE HIGHEST OF PRORITIES (John 8:55).
8. GLORIFY GOD IN ATTITUDE AND ACTION (John 8:49; 11:4; 17:4).
9. TALK WITH GOD…A LOT (John 17:1, 10).

That's how to live a life that matters—a life of significance, a life that makes a difference in this world and in our day-to-day lives. There is a better way to approach and finish life than what we've been led to believe. It's better to slide through the gates of heaven, out of breath, exhausted, "used up, worn out, leaking oil, shouting 'GERONIMO!!'" than to crawl through the gates of eternity like a puppy, whipped and whining, with its tail between its legs.

George Whitefield, the 18th Century revivalist, said, "I'd rather burn out than rust out."[17] I'm not interested in excessive busyness with no purpose or meaning—spinning my wheels and going

---

[17] Zeke Zeiler, Burn out or rust out, *Living in Light of Eternity*, May 15, 2022, retrieved from https://www.zekezeiler.com/2022/05/burn-out-or-rust-out.html#:~:text=As%20it%20turns%20out%2C%20George,a%20span%20of%2033%20years.

nowhere fast. Like Whitefield, I am consumed with the idea of commitment, dedication, and devotion to living like Jesus did—invested in people, in ministry, in *The Old Rugged Cross*, and in the kingdom of God, living a life that truly matters. No half way efforts in that regard are sufficient. No hedging your bets or straddling the theological fence like some do, one foot serving and trusting God and His word, and the other planted in an errant worldview that is antagonistic to the gospel. *"No one can serve two masters"* (Matthew 6:24, TLT). You must make a choice: Live superficially with no view of eternity, or live all-in, as God designed us to live with meaning and purpose. Live for Him, or don't. *"Choose today whom you will serve"* (Joshua 24:15, NLT). That's how life was always meant to be lived.

Be authentic. Be real. Live under the authority of God. Know, love, and live God's Word. Engage the world with the truth of the Gospel. Find and fulfill the purpose of God for your life. Live in His presence. Get to know God deeper. Glorify His name in attitude and action, and for heaven's sake, and for your own well-being, pray. Pray without ceasing about everything.

Let the revolution begin… You can live a life that matters.

> *"To repent is not to look downwards at my own shortcomings, but upwards at God's love; it is not to look backwards with self-reproach but forward with trustfulness; it is to see not what I have failed to be — but what by the grace of Christ I might yet become.*[18]
>
> **—St John Climacus (579-649 AD),**
> *Byzantine monk and author of* The Ladder of Divine Ascent.

---

[18] Jonathan R. Baily, François Fénelon: daily deaths destroy the final death, *The Inward Odessey*, https://www.jonathanrbailey.com/p/francois-fenelon-daily-deaths-destroy January 4, 2024, retrieved from

Chapter 1

THE AUTHENTIC CHRISTIAN LIFE

A Masterpiece In The Making

> **John 3:3, 5, AMPC–** *"Jesus answered him (Nicodemus), 'I assure you, most solemnly I tell you, that unless a person is born again (anew, from above), he cannot ever see (know, be acquainted with, and experience) the kingdom of God...most solemnly I tell you, unless a man is born of water and [even] the Spirit, he cannot [ever] enter the kingdom of God.'"*

Some time ago, I stumbled across a short, rather pointed and challenging verse that's been around for many years. Nobody knows who wrote it, but it reveals the true nature of Christianity—how God views and values the Christian life and the Christian, and how He might evaluate my life and yours as we move through each day. It goes like this:

> *I counted dollars while God counted crosses.*
> *I counted gains while He counted losses.*

> *I counted my worth by the things gained in store,*
> *But He sized me up by the scars that I bore.*
> *I coveted honors and sought for degrees.*
> *He wept as He counted the hours on my knees.*
> *And I never knew till one day at a grave*
> *How vain are the things that we spend life to save.*

That's convicting. The words cut *"deep into (my) innermost thoughts and desires"* (Hebrews 12:12, NLT). They are incredibly insightful, reminding me just how terribly important is the manner in which I live and practice life on a daily basis. "A man is great not because he hasn't failed," said Confucius, "a man is great because failure hasn't stopped him." An astute principle when considering the claims of genuine Christianity. Personal failure cannot stop the gospel from doing its divine, transformative work in my life.

Former Alabama head football coach Nick Saban (with seven national championships to his credit) was asked about his recent (2024) retirement. Looking back over an illustrious career, he responded, "It's not just about how many games we won and lost, but it's about the legacy and how we went about it. We always tried to do it the right way."[19] I might say the same thing about living out the Christian life on a daily basis—How we go about it and doing it the right way matters big time.

The Scriptures teach that I am to be "redeemed far down in (my) heart" [20] if we are to be counted among those who go by the name Christian. Jesus insisted that we must first be *"born from above,"* the starting point where my spiritual journey is jump-started, and

---

[19] *CNN This Morning*, January 11, 2024, retrieved from https://archive.org/details/CNNW_20240111_120000_CNN_This_Morning/start/0/end/60.

[20] Cornelius Plantinga Jr., *Engaging God's World: A Christian Vision of Faith, Learning, and Living*, (Grand Rapids, Michigan, William B. Eerdmans Publishing Company, 2002), 108.

authentic Christianity follows. The entire process is orchestrated by the *"extraordinary compassion,"* the *"extravagant mercy,"* and the *"overpowering love"* of God (Titus 3:4-5, TPT), which regenerates and renews spiritually dead men and women.

A new life emerges—a new beginning, a new purpose, a new set of spiritual eyes, new values, new direction, and a new power *"born from above"* to live successfully and victoriously as God intends. If you want to be authentic, genuine, and real in your Christian faith, and empowered to walk the Christian life, it all starts there—*"born from above"* in order to *"see"* and *"enter the kingdom of God"* (John 3:3, 5, AMPC). It is a must.

First, I must recognize my need for a Savior. I am flawed, *"dead in my trespasses and sins… following the course and fashion of this world [...this present age], following the prince of the power of the air"* (Ephesians 2:1-2). I stand as a *"helpless… sinner…(an) enemy"* of God (Romans 5:6-10, NET), a rebel at heart. My sin is forever before me, and I cannot escape the guilt for what I've done deliberately and foolheartedly. I run, weeping, to the only place I know where the rich mercy and grace of God are poured out on an undeserving man—that's me. I fall prostrate under the shadow of the *Old Rugged Cross,* where the Lamb of God, Christ Jesus, shed His blood on my behalf for the forgiveness of my sin and yours. The past is buried and gone. My blunders and poor decisions are forgotten, and yesterday's failures are no longer remembered in heaven. The gift of eternal life, secured by Christ's death and resurrection, is now offered by God and received by me in faith and trust in His work alone. He has *"made (me and you)… alive together with Christ"* (Ephesians 2:5, NET), empowered and equipped with the potential and promise for a better tomorrow in this world and a rich future reaching far into eternity. Heaven awaits the true Christian.

Ray Stedman wrote in his classic, *Authentic Christianity*:

> The authentic Christian life is essentially and radically different from the natural life lived by a man or woman...Life is lived by means of Him. Christ is a part of every wholesome action, the corrector of every wrong deed or thought, the giver of joy, and the healer of hurt. No longer merely on the edges of life, Christ is the center of everything. Life revolves around him. As a consequence, life comes into proper focus. Despite outward trials, a deep peace possesses the heart, strength grips the spirit, and kindness and joy radiate abroad. This is really living![21]

Of course, it is—life without hypocrisy. No façade. No veneer. No superficiality. Just spiritual and personal integrity, honesty, reliability, truthfulness, and maturity. "The Real McCoy"—the man or woman who has *"died to sin… (in order to) walk in newness of life"* (Romans 6:2-4).

C.H. Spurgeon wrote:

> There must be an entire and radical change of man's nature...the Gospel does not flinch from this, but enforces the declaration. The Holy Spirit does not attempt to improve human nature into something better, but lays the axe at the root of the trees and declares that we must become (and will become) new

---

[21] Ray Stedman, Authentic Christianity, (Portland, Oregon: Multnomah Press, 1974), 161-162.

creatures—and that by a supernatural work of the Omnipotent God...[22]

Authenticity is miraculous. Grace makes it certain. U2 lead singer, Bono, said of his own Christian experience:

> Your nature is a hard thing to change; it takes time.... I have heard of people who have life-changing, miraculous turnarounds, people set free from addiction after a single prayer, relationships saved where both parties "let go, and let God."
>
> But it was not like that for me. For all that "I was lost, I am found," it is probably more accurate to say, "I was really lost. I'm a little less so at the moment." And then a little less, and a little less again.
>
> That, to me, is the spiritual life. The slow reworking and rebooting the computer at regular intervals, reading the small print of the service manual. It has slowly rebuilt me in a better image (the *image of the Son*, Jesus). It has taken years, though, and it is not over yet..[23]

I would fully concur. Transformation seems to come quickly in some cases, but mostly it appears to be a slow process in many others. Crucifixion is a slow, agonizing death, but it must come, and it will come by divine power to each of us until God has finished the work He began in my life and yours (Philippians 1:6).

---

[22] C.H. Spurgeon, in a sermon he preached in August 1873, Retrieved from https://www.ccel.org/ccel/spurgeon/sermons19.xli.html.
[23] U2 and Neil McCormick, *U2 by U2*, (Bishopsbriggs, Glasgow: HarperCollins, 2006), 7.

The Christian life is designed to be lived successfully, productively, and progressively (sanctification) to make a good showing of ourselves before the world. God is the only Source from which we can draw our strength to yield a "fruit-bearing," God-honoring life and live in a manner that is pleasing to Him. The call to follow Christ is to join Jesus in acting redemptively, sacrificing our own agenda, and ultimately surrendering our will to the purpose and plan of God—something none of us are particularly inclined to do. Frankly, we sometimes prefer a bobble head, plastic Jesus shaking his head yes to every whim. A Jesus with no real punch, making no real moral demands and serving no true purpose other than rocking and swaying side-to-side on the dashboard of our car as we move through life. Submission to heaven's authority over our lives is not easy, but it is the mark of authentic Christianity and living a life that truly matters. I must have the "real thing."

All self-interests must be placed on the altar of sacrifice, at the cross of Christ, where the inner, self-serving man must come to an end. My attitudes, thoughts, and motives must be buried, like the *"seed"* Jesus spoke about that cannot bear fruit unless it first dies (John 12:24-26). Ken Winters, author, retired pastor, and vice president at IMB (the Southern Baptist International Missions Board), put it like this:

> I've never thought about seeds needing to die. To me, seeds have always been the picture of new life just bursting to get out. But the fact of the matter is that the seed must die in order for life to burst out. As it dies, it transforms into roots that go deep, and stems that soon make their way out of the dirt into the air in order to grow and blossom.[24]

---

[24] Ken Winters, A seed must die, *Ken Winter Blog*, September 9, 2020, retrieved from https://kenwinter.org/blog/a-seed-must-die.

Self-promotion, prestige, possessions, and the preservation of the self at any cost—including my self-esteem, self-interests, self-concern, self-absorption, self-centeredness, and self-satisfaction, etc. must all go. Not just simply removed, but inevitably terminated, becoming rubble, and reduced to unequivocal ruin, dead, buried, and gone for good. *"Follow Me,"* Jesus demanded. He offered no qualifiers, except one: "When Christ calls a man, he bids him come and die."[25] Sobering words from Dietrich Bonhoeffer, who was executed in a Nazi prison near the end of World War II.

In 62 AD, Paul reminded Titus, who was living in Crete, a city notorious for its moral decadence,

> **Titus 2:11-13, PHILLIPS** – "*...to have no more to do with godlessness or the desires of this world* (a significant change was expected) *but to live, here and now, responsible, honorable and God-fearing lives...For he* (Jesus) *gave himself for us all, that he might rescue us from all our evil ways and make for himself a people of his own, clean and pure, with our hearts set upon living a life that is good.*

"Our lives have become earthly in orientation and fleshly in operation," wrote James Emery White, senior pastor and former adjunct professor and president of Gordon-Conwell Theological Seminary,

> We conform to the patterns of the world, when we could be morphed into the very image of Christ (Romans 12:1-2). We focus on religion instead of relationship. Practice instead of passion. Such a life–not rooted in an authentic relationship with God, full

---

[25] Dietrich Bonhoeffer, *The Cost of Discipleship*, (New York, NY: Simon and Schuster, 1995), 89.

of rhetoric and posturing, form and mannerism – is all but empty. We become people possessed with knowledge 'about' as opposed to an acquaintance 'with.' But only an intimate relationship with the living God leads to true spirituality. And only true spirituality can affect the world. [26]

That's transformational living.

Hymnist, Mary Brown, captured the essence of an authentic life.

It may not be on the mountain's height,
Or over the stormy sea;
It may not be at the battle's front
My Lord will have need of me;
But if by a still, small voice He calls
To paths I do not know,
I'll answer, dear Lord, with my hand in Thine,
I'll go where You want me to go…
I'll be what you want me to be.[27]

That's genuine, real, authentic Christian living. It can happen. It should happen. It must happen, for it is God, *"the Spirit living within you,"* who *"gives you* (and me) *life"* (Romans 8:9-10, NLT)—a legitimate, spiritual life, a life supernaturally enabled and spiritually endowed to follow Christ and His calling. Nothing else can produce genuine Christianity and a life worth living. Absolutely nothing.

Not my will. It is not strong enough, nor is it free enough to make the right decisions and choices in life. The will is insufficient

---

[26] James Emery White, *Serious Times: Making Your Life Matter in an Urgent Day*, (Downers Grove, Illinois, 2004), 80.
[27] Mary Brown, I'll Go Where You Want Me to Go, Public Domain.

in and of itself. Paul's words to the church at Rome indict the entire human race: *"No one seeks God... all have turned away... no one does good"* (Romans 3:11-12, ESV). We do not have the fortitude or the inclination to go as far as making God's will our will. No man or woman can generate such willpower on their own—such abandonment, such sacrifice, such consistency of heart, soul, and mind to be completely given over to God. Left to our own devices, *"we all fall short of God's glorious standard"* (Romans 3:23, NLT). No man or woman will willingly climb the scaffold to be burned at the stake for his or her faith or be crucified upside down alongside Peter (John 21:18). Apart from the infusion of God-given guidance and divine power into one's spiritual veins, the will of humankind is inadequate.

It's not my faith that will keep me afloat when I *"pass through the waters,"* but God, my *"Savior,"* who *"created"* me, *"formed"* me, and *"redeemed"* me (Isaiah 43:1-3, NIV). My faith is seriously lacking. One might say it's unreliable, defective, and erratic at best, especially when the pressure is on and my life has gone south. It can't be my beliefs that will rescue me. At best, they are muddied and unclear, susceptible to change, and *"carried about,"* warned Paul, *"by every wind of doctrine, by the trickery of men, by craftiness in deceitful scheming"* (Ephesians 4:14). And certainly, I can't depend on my intellect, for I am not as sharp or as smart as I think I am, especially when I'm trying to figure out God—what He's up to and/or what He requires of me.

Something else, or better yet, Someone else (God Himself), must be at work in my life and yours to bring about authenticity. He gives a rebellious heart (like mine and yours) the "want-to," the drive, the will, the wisdom, and even the faith to fully commit to Christ. It's the grace of God that ultimately gets the job done. *"For by grace you have been saved* (perfect tense—completed action with ongoing positive results) [28] *through faith"* (Ephesians 2:8-9). D.L. Moody said, "I'm glad we are saved by grace, not by good works, (not my good faith, not my strong will, nor my high I.Q., or anything else for that matter). Because I don't wanna sit in heaven and listen to everybody brag for eternity about how they got there."[29] I couldn't agree more. I'd rather boast *"in the cross of our Lord Jesus Christ, through which the world has been crucified to me, and I to the world"* (Galatians 6:14).

One-time president of Dallas Theological Seminary, Charles Swindoll, spoke to students preparing for ministry. He quoted a prayer of commitment from an unknown source. When I read it, I thought, "That is the very essence, the very foundation upon which I can and must build a life that matters and live authentically in the power of the Spirit of God." It reads,

> Lord,
> I am willing to receive what You give.
> I am willing to lack what You withhold.
> I am willing to relinquish what You take.
> I am willing to suffer what You inflict.

Every word of that prayer screams grace and authenticity. That's how I want to see my life move forward—a Spirit-led willingness and conformity to live like it matters by the grace of God, making my days count with every sunrise, few though they may be, or as many as God sees fit to give me.

---

[28] Benejamin Chapman, New Testament-Greek Notebook, (Grand Rapids, Michigan: Baker Book House, 1977), 66, 69.
[29] D.L. Moody, Facebook post, *Carry the Light,* February 10, 2024, retrieved from https://www.facebook.com/story.php?story_fbid=707435504833933&id=1000670246863 33&mibextid=oFDknk.

John Wooden, arguably the greatest college basketball coach of all time, put it like this to his son: "Make each day your masterpiece."[30] That's it! The Apostle Paul agrees.

> **Ephesians 2:10, AMPC** - *"For we are God's [own] handiwork (His workmanship), recreated in Christ Jesus, [born anew] that we may do those good works which God predestined (planned beforehand) for us [taking paths which He prepared ahead of time], that we should walk in them [living the good life which He prearranged and made ready for us to live]."*

Clearly, it does matter how you and I live (Ephesians 2:4-10). Vitor Belfort won his first Ultimate Fighting Championship match in twelve seconds of the first round. His entire fighting career was ahead of him following his victory over John Hess. Belfort said, "I told God that if I won that fight, I would serve Him forever. But I didn't keep my promise." He was anything but authentic. He continued, "I bargained with God. It was all about me and what I wanted. It took me thirteen years to understand that to be a follower of Jesus, I need to die every day. I needed to kill myself daily."[31] Of course, he was speaking of his own agenda, attitudes, and actions. It all had to go if he was to find happiness, fulfillment, and contentment.

He later sustained a neck injury that threatened his career and future. His sister was kidnapped and never came home. He was devastated. He admitted, "I was losing my faith. I was so mad. I wanted revenge. My heart started to get hard… I was bitter. I was hurt."[32] He was in pain, agonizing over the loss of his sister and the

---

[30] Craig Impelman, Make each day your masterpiece, *Success Presents*, Jan 18, 2017, retrieved from https://www.thewoodeneffect.com/your-masterpiece/.
[31] Doug Bender and Dave Sterrett, *I Am Second: Real Stories. Changed Lives*, (Nashville, Tennessee, 2012), 112.
[32] Ibid, 115.

potential loss of his future in the UFC. A pastor told him that he needed to "trust God and give Him your life." Good advice for all flesh and blood.

Belfort admitted, "I was just a religious man looking for answers and help. I was so selfish. I didn't want to give anything to God. I just wanted Him to fix everything… I finally started to understand that I needed a relationship with Jesus, not a religion. I need His mercy, grace, and love." Now, that's honest. That's real. That's authentic.

If you want the Christian experience, *"You must be born again."* That's where the journey of a lifetime truly happens. Vitor Belfort revealed his secret: "I choose to make God first, and I am doing my best to make that a reality in my life. I choose to live second."[33] That's real. That's genuine. That's how authentic Christianity was meant to work.

---

[33] Ibid, 116.

"More men fail through lack of purpose than lack of talent."
— **Billy Sunday**

Chapter 2

LIVE UNDER THE AUTHORITY OF GOD

John 8:42 AMPC *"I proceeded (came forth) from God [out of His very presence]. I did not even come on My own authority or of My own accord (as self-appointed); but He sent Me."*

John 12:49-50, MSG *"I'm not making any of this up on my own. The Father who sent me gave me orders, told me what to say and how to say it. And I know exactly what his command produces: real and eternal life. That's all I have to say. What the Father told me, I tell you."*

— *Jesus*

Michael Jordan, one of the best—if not the greatest—NBA basketball players to ever lace up a pair of Nike sneakers and step onto the court, was once asked what he thought his best skill was. He didn't say it was his ability to dunk from the free-throw line or his scoring prowess. His answer was simply, "I was coachable. I was a sponge and aggressive to learn. The easier you are to lead, the further you'll go."[34]

And so it is when I live under the authority of God. It matters who is running—or ruining—my life. It matters whether I am "coachable." It matters whether I am willing to surrender my preferences in approaching daily life or if I am able to adopt God's ways and learn from Him how to face the day.

The early church father, Saint John Chrysostom (347–407 AD), was not always a saint. He said of his youth that he "plunged into the whirlpool of the world" (been there). Later, he was converted to Christianity and became the Archbishop of Constantinople in 397 AD after twelve years of service as a humble priest. His oratory skills were extraordinary. "Chrysostom" means "golden-mouth," and apparently, he was all of that and a bag of chips when he entered the pulpit. He was fearless in declaring the Scriptures to both commoners and nobility alike, unafraid to denounce the morals and ill behavior of those failing to live out the gospel in their daily lives. Consequently, he was anything but popular and was threatened with execution and eventually banished from Constantinople. He was escorted out of the city under military guard and never returned.[35] So be it. He would not cave to intimidation. He held his ground, dug in, and stubbornly refused to surrender to any authority in his life other than Christ and His word. He said this.

> What can I fear? Will it be death? But you know that Christ is my life, and that I shall gain by death. Will it be exile? But the

---

[34] Arjun Julka, 10 x Scoring Champion Michael Jordan once admitted how donning the role of a 'sponge' was his greatest skill, *The Sports Rush, NBA News*, December 04, 2022, retrieved from https://thesportsrush.com/nba-news-10x-scoring-champion-michael-jordan-once-admitted-how-donning-the-role-of-a-sponge-was-his-greatest-skill/.

[35] Editors, John Chrysostom: Legendary Early Church Preacher, *Church History Institute*, Issue 44, Retrieved from https://christianhistoryinstitute.org/uploaded/50cf81a8ba3640.51540582.pdf.

earth and all its fullness is the Lord's. Will it be the loss of wealth? But we brought nothing into the world, and can carry nothing out. Thus, all the terrors of the world are contemptible in my eyes, and I smile at all its good things. Poverty I do not fear. Riches I do not sigh for. Death I do not shrink from.[36]

Here was a man who lived like it mattered. In fact, he lived as if the only thing that mattered was Christ—his daily walk with Him and the ministry God called him to do.

Living under God's authority means that God alone holds the highest priority. He has absolute, unquestionable, sovereign rule and power over every facet of my personal, daily life. No holdouts. He calls the shots. He presides over every minute of every day. He has the right and the ability to decree, to order, to declare, to have charge over my affairs and interfere with my agenda, my aspirations, and alter my belief systems. As the Creator and King of all things *"in the heavens and on earth, visible and invisible, whether thrones or dominions or rulers or authorities—all things have been created through Him and for Him"* (Colossians 1:16), it is to His authority that I must bend the knee, cling to His royal robe, and not let go, no matter what. *"He must increase, but I must decrease"* (John 3:30, ESV)—simple yet profound words to live by and govern my life. John the Baptist knew his place in this world and the next. He said that he was not fit to untie the sandals of Jesus (John 1:27), a declaration of submission and surrender to the authority and throne of God.

During the early charismatic movement of the 1970s, I got to know a fellow pastor in the community where I served the local church. He was a delightful, gentle-spirited man who loved God and

---

[36] Editors, The fear of man, *Ministry 127,* No date, retrieved from https://ministry127.com/resources/illustration/the-fear-of-man.

the people he served. On occasion, we would share pastoral duties together, visit the hospital together, pray together, share Christ, minister to the needy, and talk theology. I loved our time together. Eventually, the man died of cancer, leaving behind a wife and several children. Unfortunately, before his death, he had vacated his pulpit and surrendered his position as pastor. He left the ministry under pressure from members of his own congregation, who embraced the *"priesthood of believers"* to the extreme. They no longer felt the need for a pastor. In essence, they demoted him, dismissed him, and discounted his calling to the pastoral ministry. I could see the confusion in his eyes as we talked. So, I challenged him.

"Let no one rob you of God's calling upon your life," I said, "to the pastoral ministry or anywhere or anything else for that matter. Nor should you discount the anointing of God for the role that was divinely assigned to you and you alone or lay it aside for a lesser position and task in this world. No man or organization has that authority to undo what God has ordained in eternity past. Unless God has informed you otherwise, you must do what He has commanded you to do in the time and place of His choosing. The last time I checked, the sovereign God of the universe does not make mistakes. Nor does He change His mind so easily, if ever. Stay the course for which you have been ordered and directed by heaven. There are no other options, but to live and serve under God's authority.

Live like it matters, with or without man's approval, beneath heaven's divine appointment.

Moses left the safety of the Midian desert for the palace halls of Egypt to confront the likes of Pharaoh. Sent by God, he had his mission and his work cut out for him—*"bring God's people, the sons of Israel, out of Egypt"* (Exodus 3:10). So, he packed up his things and went to the courts of a pagan country and declared without compromise God's word. He lived and breathed the authority of God. So must you and I, if we want our lives to count.

"When the day of evil comes (and it is already here)... *stand your ground (rooted in the rich soil of God's word and will), and after you have done everything, to stand"* (Ephesians 6:13, NIV). The authority of God, His word, precepts, and life principles are necessities for living a life that matters. Life works when His authority prevails over all things, *"that He Himself might come to have first place in everything"* (Colossians 1:18).

Stand your ground for righteousness and right living. Stand for holiness, purity, and integrity. Stand for the cross, for *"the way, the truth, and the life"* (John 14:6). Stand your ground before the school board in your community and demand a quality education that includes the God of creation. Stand up for teachers who are diligent and committed to teaching reading, writing, and arithmetic, who will accurately teach the lessons of history, including positive morals and family values. Stand on the authority of God for marriage between a man and a woman. Stand on the foundation of God's word for sexuality designed by God. Stand in the halls of justice and demand that our children be protected from all manner of predators. Stand for the sanctity of life. Stand for the dignity of men and women created in the image of God. Stand firm *"against all strategies of the devil"* (Ephesians 6:11).

The disciples did just that. A man who had been lame for forty years was healed "in *the name of Jesus"* (Acts 3:16, NLT). It was an extraordinary miracle witnessed by many. Word spread throughout Jerusalem about what had taken place. Peter and John stood before the crowd that had gathered and spoke about *"faith"* in Christ (Acts 3:16), *"the authority of Jesus"* (Acts 4:2, NLT), and "the *resurrection of the dead"* (Acts 4:2, NLT). They were jailed and dragged before the religious leaders of the day to answer for their behavior. *"By what power or in whose name* (authority) *have you done this?"* (Acts 4:7, NLT). The question was not only about power but about authorization. Who gave them the right to act? The answer was Jesus. They were warned to say nothing further, but they were under God's orders and authority to speak the truth. They would not, nor could they, remain silent. *"There is salvation in no one else"* (Acts 4:12, NLT). Peter and John asked their interrogators, *"Do you think God wants us to obey you rather than him? We cannot stop telling about the wonderful things we have seen and heard"* (Acts 4:19, NLT). Heaven trumps human authorities and opinions every time. His word and will take precedence over all else. This is a principle the church and its members must recapture in this day and age.

Jesus set the pace for those who would follow Him. From the time He was a boy, He lived under the authority of God, His Father. He ministered and spoke with divine authorization and expertise (Matthew 7:29). So must we, as disciples of Christ. He served with distinction and divine unction to fulfill the single purpose for which He was sent. He willingly took on the responsibility of completing the tasks of redemption and the role of Redeemer, for which He left the palaces of heaven to come to planet Earth. He could not and would not be persuaded by clever logic or convinced by hell's arguments and pressures to change the course of His life or lay down His mantle as prophet, king, and priest. Even after forty days in the Judean desert—hungry, thirsty, and physically weakened—Jesus would not cower or give in to the devil's temptations. He stood His ground. He had a mandate from heaven. His mind was made up. His face was resolute. His conviction was sure. He was *the Lamb of God, the Great I AM, the Resurrection and the Life, the Light of the world, the Bread of life,* and nobody or no one was going to tell Him otherwise or stop Him. He set His face toward fulfilling His divine destiny, answerable to God the Father alone. He defined His life on the authority of God. Maybe we should do likewise and avoid *"seeing things merely from a human point of view"* (Matthew 16:21-23, NLT), a practice that has often gotten me into trouble.

Authority—particularly God's—is about His indisputable right to command and control. After all, *"The earth is the Lord's"* (Exodus 9:29, NIV). His throne oversees the universe and beyond (Isaiah 66:1). Upon His head sits the crown of *"glory and honor"* (Hebrews 12:2). In His hand, He holds the *"scepter of righteousness"* (Hebrews 1:8) and possesses all authority and power to do as He pleases (Matthew 28:18), including the command of my life and the life of a nation.

Some years ago, the Chicago Tribune (May 20, 2002) carried the story of 23-year-old Army Specialist Jeff Lewis. Lewis was a supply clerk with the 82nd Airborne Division. Unexpectedly, he received orders—probably due to a clerical error—to parachute jump without any preparation or formal training. This was his first jump out the door of an airplane. Without question or hesitation, he did what he was ordered to do. Fortunately, he landed unhurt. He later said he was just doing what a good soldier is supposed to do—follow orders. "The Army said I was airborne-qualified," Lewis said. "I wasn't going to question it."[37] And neither should we when God orders our steps and changes the course of our lives. He doesn't err. He doesn't screw things up. I can do that without any help from above.

God has the right to rule and to reign, to make decisions—whether I understand them or not. His orders are unquestionable. He

---

[37] Editors, Radical trust and obedience, *Preaching Today*, retrieved from https://www.preachingtoday.com/illustrations/2000/october/12675.html.

governs as He sees fit. He demands respect from His subjects and expects full compliance with His word and will. In other words, what He says goes. His word is final. His decisions are binding.

Jesus served under the authority of God the Father. He stood—and stands—in the Father's place in this world, above all sickness and disease, over every storm unleashed in my daily life. The waves of the sea are subject to His desires. The unfolding of human history, including my life and yours, is directed by God's purpose. Even the demons of hell bow before His majesty and *"shudder in terror and horror such as (to) make a man's hair stand on end"* (James 2:19, AMPC). He is the ultimate boss, in charge of my life and yours. His word has the final say in all matters of faith and practice. All of creation and every creature fall under His jurisdiction. His decisions are straightforward and binding from eternity past and on into the future. Never will a word that *"goes out from (God's) mouth… return to (Him) empty, but will accomplish what (He) desires and achieve the purpose for which (He) sent it"* (Isaiah 55:11, NIV), and that applies to my personal, daily life. It is secure in the "unimpeachable authority" of Christ.[38]

Max Lucado wrote,

> The Roman government tried to intimidate him (Jesus). False religion tried to silence him. The Devil tried to kill him. All failed. Even "death was no match for him" (Acts 2:24, MSG). He was not kidding when he declared, "All authority in heaven and earth has been given to me (Matthew 11:27, NIV).[39]

---

[38] Max Lucado, January 6, Unimpeachable authority, *God is With You Every day: A 365-Day Devotional*, (Nashville, Tennessee: Thomas Nelson, 2015), January 6.
[39] Ibid.

The authority of God was the very reason Abram left his home, his *"native country,"* his *"relatives,"* and his *"father's family"* behind—because God told him to do just that (Genesis 12:1, NLT). God ordered it, and Abram carried out the will of God for his life. There was never any real choice. Abram got his mission (I've got mine, and you've got yours). This was never a suggestion. It was a directive straight from the mouth of God Himself. Literally—*"Get out!"* No options here. No questions asked… just pack up, move out, and get your butt going. Abram did what he was told, *"as the Lord had spoken to him"* (Genesis 12:4). He moved. He changed the course of his life on the authority of God's word—simply because God said so. That's it. No argument. No bargaining. No negotiating. God was now orchestrating his affairs.

Abram didn't need to know why, where, how, or even when. I often do, but he didn't. He was sure of only one thing, and it was enough. God spoke greatness into his life, *and "Abraham believed in (trusted in) God, and it was credited to his account as righteousness (right decision, right living, and right standing with God)"* (Romans 4:3, AMPC). So, the man left yesterday behind and *"journeyed on"* (Genesis 12:9), under the authority of God, setting his eyes in faith toward the horizon to a place he knew not. He did so, believing that his life would count for more than minding his father's store (who made and sold idols), herding sheep, and pitching tents as a nomad in the desert. His life would matter. His name would be *"great,"* and his life would become a *"blessing"* to many (Genesis 12:1-3)—to more people than he could have ever imagined, numbering like the stars of the heavens (Genesis 15:5). Who would have thought the life of one man would count for so much? Thousands of years later, he would become *"the father of a multitude of nations"* (Genesis 17:4-5). If Abram had failed to leave home as instructed, none of this would have happened. But it did, because he lived out his life under God's authority—and that matters.

When God speaks, we listen (or at least, we should). He commands, we obey—and we do so with hearts surrendered to His will, with faith in His word, and confidence in His wisdom, character, and power. *"Thus saith the Lord"* means snap to attention, prepare yourself to receive orders and instructions from on high, and get ready to carry out *"every word that proceeds from the mouth of God"* (Matthew 4:4, NKJV). So must it be for you and me if we ever hope to live a successful life that truly matters.

Nehemiah was such a man. He asked God to *"send"* him back to Jerusalem, a city in ruins (Nehemiah 2:5), with the express purpose of rebuilding its walls (Nehemiah 2:5-20). And so he went and started the repairs, but soon faced great opposition from those who would stop the divinely commissioned project and discredit the man leading the work. The pressure was on. The opposition was relentless. False news was real. Some things don't ever change. But God's man had an ace up his sleeve. His decisions were justified. His actions were warranted... because *"the good hand of my God was on me"* (Nehemiah 2:8)—the secret to victorious living and spiritual power. *"My God,"* said Nehemiah, *"was putting into my mind (what) to do for Jerusalem"* (Nehemiah 2:12). He knew what the King wanted. The sovereign God spoke, and Nehemiah moved forward without hesitation, with confidence, courage, and peace of mind. He had God's approval to serve heaven's interests. He functioned and worked under the authority of God, which gave him the guts not to quit and the determination to march ahead until the task was finished, regardless of the opposition. Nehemiah lived like it mattered, and fifty-two days later, the wall was completed (Nehemiah 6:15). He stayed the course. He did not back down. The outcome was predictable—success, achievement, and victory, all realized for doing and being all that God had in mind. The authority of God gets results. It always has. It always will.

God has also called you and divinely equipped you for a particular role in this world, just as He did with Nehemiah and so many others throughout history. You have your place, your path, and the blessing of God. I have mine. You must not ignore His holy directions or lay aside God's calling upon your life. That call is an essential part of who you are as a follower and disciple of Christ and a participant in His gospel.

In the introduction to his book *What Jesus Demands from the World,* John Piper wrote about the Christian life and the authority of Jesus to command His followers to *"make disciples,"* and fulfill the great commission. Piper noted the necessity of our relationship with Christ as we move through each day in obedience to His word and will.

> On one side he (Jesus) says, "All authority in heaven and on earth has been given to me" (Matt. 28:18). And on the other side he says, "Behold, I am with you always, to the end of the age" (Matt. 28:20). The one says, "I make demands because I have the right. All authority in the universe is mine." The other says, "I make demands because I will help you (do what I want you to do and be what you must be to complete the task assigned to you by Me). I will be with you forever."[40]

A great truth that will carry you and me far in this life and into the world to come.

---

[40] John Piper, What Jesus Demands from the World, (Wheaton, Illinois: Crossway, 2006), 25.

Joe Mazzulla, the head coach of the 2024 NBA Champions, the Boston Celtics, spoke of his journey back in December 2023, months before the playoffs.

> I know that for my wife, my family, and me, we're supposed to be here. For us, our faith is really important, and we felt like we followed God's plan to a T as to where He wanted us to be.[41]

Smart man, living and walking under the authority of God's providence. On the court before a national audience immediately following the championship game, ESPN's Lisa Salters asked Mazzulla why this time was the right time for the Celtics to advance to the NBA Finals. He didn't hesitate. He said, "It's just where God has us right now. We're all exactly where we're supposed to be…" [42] The authority and power of God at work in your life and mine—serving and functioning under God's orders, stamped "Approved" for this time, in this place, for this task—to live out a life that truly matters. In the words of the great philosopher, Larry the Cable Guy, "Git r done!"

---

[41] Kevin Mercer Joe Mazzulla following 'God's plan' as he coaches Celtics in NBA playoffs, *Sports Spectrum*, May 3, 2023, retrieved from https://sportsspectrum.com/sport/basketball/2023/05/03/joe-mazzulla-gods-plan-coach-celtics-playoffs/ .

[42] Kevin Mercer, Head coach Joe Mazzulla leads Celtics back to NBA Finals, says it's 'where God has us,' *Sports Spectrum*, May 28, 2024, retrieved from https://sportsspectrum.com/sport/basketball/2024/05/28/joe-mazzulla-celtics-nba-finals-where-god-has-us/.

I am a Christian because God says so, and I did what he told me to do, and I stand on God's Word, and if the Book goes down, I'll go with it.

— **Billy Sunday**

Chapter 3

WALK DAILY IN THE LIGHT OF GOD'S WORD

John 8:12, PHILLIPS - *"I am the light of the world. The man who follows me will never walk in the dark but will live his life in the light."*

John 8:31-32 - *"If you abide in My word, then you are truly disciples if Mine, and you shall know the truth and the truth shall make you free."*

John 17:17 - *"Thy word is truth"*

After winning the speakership in the Fall of 2023, Republican Mike Johnson told Fox News "that his Christian faith is central to his personal identity." Imagine that from a politician.

He said,

> *I am a Bible-believing Christian. Someone asked me today in the media, they said, "It's curious, people are curious. What does Mike Johnson think about any issue under the sun?" I said, "Well, go pick up a*

Bible off your shelf and read it—that's my worldview. That's what I believe, and so I make no apologies for it.[43]

Good for him. May that man's tribe increase.

In a politically charged environment where blatant secularism reigns supreme, Johnson's character and faith came under attack. Nothing new here. Some called him a "religious fundamentalist," while others likened him to a Middle Eastern terrorist or a mass murderer. However, Mike Johnson stood his ground. He did not back down. He firmly believed that the key to successful, life-changing, power-packed Christian living is knowing the Scriptures and placing them at the core of daily living and every decision life throws his way (including at the ballot box and beyond*).* Jesus said (not my words, but His), *"Anyone who belongs to God listens gladly to the words of God"* (John 9:47, NLT). Not so in a culture that promotes itself as a know-it-all, self-indulgent, self-defining, anything-goes worldview system. Sadly, some churches reflect the current culture and have failed to imitate Christ, uphold biblical values and principles, and mirror the person and Word of God.

The world, as we have come to know it, has done its very best to redline the very existence of God from daily living. No interaction or influence with the divine is tolerated. It is the Garden of Eden all over again, where people discount the Word of God. The Scriptures have been disavowed. In short, God has been "X'd" out of nearly every aspect of life. That matters—or at least it should matter—to

---

[43] Chris Enloe, Speaker Mike Johnson fights back after liberals attack his Christian faith, compare him to terrorists, *Blaze Media,* November 01, 2023, retrieved from https://www.theblaze.com/news/mike-johnson-responds-attacks-his-faith?utm_source=theblaze-breaking&utm_medium=email&utm_campaign=20231101Trending-SpeakerJohnson&utm_term=ACTIVE%20LIST%20-%20TheBlaze%20Breaking%20News.

those who want to follow Christ and advance His kingdom. Jude wrote to first-century Christians:

> **Jude 3, Phillips** - *I feel compelled to make my letter to you an earnest appeal to put up a real fight for the faith which has been once and for all committed to those who belong to Christ. For there are men who have surreptitiously entered the Church but who have for a long time been heading straight for the condemnation, I shall plainly give them. They have no real reverence for God, and they abuse his grace as an opportunity for immorality. They will not recognize the only master, Jesus Christ our Lord.*

The *"real fight for the faith"* centers around the validity, trustworthiness, and veracity of the Bible, which was designed by the God of creation to guide and govern humanity through every generation toward daily, successful living under the wisdom, grace, love, and mercy of God. "Here then is our guidebook," D.L. Moody remarked, "our textbook—the Word. If I utter a syllable that is not justified by the Scriptures, don't believe me. The Bible is the only rule. Walk by it and it alone."[44] Not bad for a former shoe salesman.

Truth stands forever. It does not change. In the opening pages of every *Gideon Bible* (over four hundred and fifty million placed and distributed) is found, what some have called "the most important description of the Bible ever written." It sums up the content and themes contained in Scripture and reads in part:

---

[44] Stanley n. Gundry, The Three Rs of Moody's Theology, Christianity Today/Christian History, Issue 25, 1990, retrieved from https://www.christianitytoday.com/history/issues/issue-25/three-rs-of-moodys-theology.html.

> The Bible contains the mind of God, the state of man, the way of salvation, the doom of sinners, and the happiness of believers. Its doctrines are holy, its precepts are binding, its histories are true, and its decisions are immutable. Read it to be wise, believe it to be safe, and practice it to be holy. It contains light to direct you, food to support you, and comfort to cheer you. It is the traveler's map, the pilgrim's staff, the pilot's compass, the soldier's sword, and the Christian's charter. Here too, Heaven is opened, and the gates of Hell disclosed. Christ is its grand subject, our good its design, and the glory of God its end…[45]

The doctrine and teachings of the Church are founded and grounded in the Word of the living God and have stood as a beacon of truth throughout the centuries. John MacArthur, pastor-teacher of Grace Community Church in Sun Valley, California, and president of The Master's College and Seminary, is considered by *Christianity Today* to be "one of the most influential preachers of his time." He rightly concluded, "There are no changing doctrines in Christianity. There are no changing values. There are no changing morals. There are no changing ethics."[46] There is no middle ground.

Joshua D. Chatraw and Mark D. Allen wrote in their book *Apologetics at the Cross* that, "Something is either true or false… If you deny that there is any such thing as 'right' and 'left' or 'north' and 'south,' it doesn't matter what type of map you draw (or use)—it won't work."[47] We will end up lost in a maze of choices, not

---

[45] Staff Writer, Religion: What's in the front of the Gideon Bible?, *Victorville Daily Press*, May 2, 2013, retrieved from https://www.vvdailypress.com/story/news/local/lucerne-valley-leader/2013/05/02/religion-what-s-in-front/24447016007/
[46] John MacArthur, A Call for Discernment, Sermon Part 2, o*Christian.com: For the Online Christian*, No date, retrieved from http://articles.ochristian.com/article2291.shtml.
[47] Joshua D. Chatraw and Mark D. Allen, *Apologetics at the Cross*, (Grand Rapids, Michigan: Zonder Academic, 2018), 184.

knowing which way to go or which one to choose. There are no reference points from which to get our bearings, and thus no sense of where we are, how to get from point A to point B, or where we are headed. We need a holy map with divine coordinates to guide us to the place of God's choosing to accomplish what He wants us to do with our lives. And that matters greatly.

Joshua started his leadership assignment at the helm of Israel. For forty years, the nation wandered in the desert because of their distrust of God and their faithlessness toward Him and His plan for their lives. God's word was ignored. As a result, an entire generation died off before God put them once again on the banks of the Jordan, ready to cross over and inhabit the land of Canaan, which He had promised to them. Before the people stood the high walls of the city of Jericho and a formidable, well-seasoned army prepared to defend it. Israel's track record was anything but stellar; they were an undependable, stubborn, and obstinate lot. Joshua would need help. He needed orders from God to achieve victory—a new perspective, new motivation, and a new resolve to carry out the battle plan in every detail according to the word of the Lord. Before Israel took a single step, before Joshua issued the order to march, he made this declaration: *"All that You (God) have commanded us, we will do, and wherever You send us, we will go"* (Joshua 1:16). Obedience to the word of God was demanded and required. It was the best decision he ever made, and it was the key to Israel's success—and ours. "The Christian lives and dies by the Book."[48]

The plan was to have a military parade with a marching band of seven priests blowing trumpets. That was it. Once each day for six days, the parade would happen. And then, on the final day, they were to take seven more trips around the outer thick walls of the city. Not

---

[48] A.W. Tozer, *The Crucified Life*, (Ada, Michigan: Bethany House, 2011),16.

a word was to be spoken. Silence was required until the command was given by Joshua to shout—perhaps to quiet the naysayers.

Honestly, the whole thing seemed ludicrous, maybe reckless from a purely human perspective. There were no field tactics to speak of. No military strategy. No counterattack measures. Nothing—just a parade with an ensemble of seven priests playing ram's horns and carrying the Ark of the Covenant. It seemed more like the Macy's Thanksgiving Day Parade than a military maneuver. Forty thousand troops *"in battle array... equipped for war"* (Joshua 4:12-13) marched before the people. No clowns. No balloons. No Santa Claus in a Christmas sleigh with a bag full of toys. This was war, plain and simple.

I'm not a battlefield general, but the plan seemed to lack military genius. Israel, however, ignored their fears, dropped their questions and doubts, and moved forward in faithful obedience as God commanded, executing the divine plan with precision. The walls of the city came crashing down, as God promised. Victory was achieved. It is always the same in the world of flesh and blood: Obedience to the Word of God is my only hope for living a life that truly matters.

Jesus said of His own life,

> **John 12:49-50** — *"I have never spoken (or acted) on My own authority or of My own accord or as self-appointed, but the Father Who sent Me has Himself given Me orders [concerning] what to say and what to tell (and what to do).*
>
> *And I know that His commandment is (means) eternal life. So whatever I speak, I am saying (and*

doing) *[exactly] what My Father has told Me to say and* (do) *in accordance with His instructions.*

Six-foot-nine, two hundred and seventy-five pound D.J. Burns played basketball for the North Carolina State University Wolfpack, the only #11 ranked team left in this year's 2024 NCAA Men's Basketball Tournament. They are playing in the "Sweet 16," for the first time since 2015. In his biography, Burns listed the priorities that govern his life. He wrote three things—: "Bible. Books. Ball." A summation of his priorities and values. Burns said, "Glory be to God. Through Him, it is always possible to overcome obstacles."[49] He and his team have done just that.

God's word was, and is, final. Put His word into action, and you get results—God's results. The core of Christ's life, every word He spoke, every step He took, was clearly based in the Scriptures. There was nothing of more value, importance, or significance outside of people themselves. Everything Jesus did rested squarely on what God the Father revealed to God the Son, directing His life toward redemption and bringing all things to their divinely appointed end. There would be no surprises. Jesus lived *"in accordance with His (Father's) instructions"* (John 12:50). The only thing that truly mattered, the only thing that moved Him, was the revelation of His Father's word. He put that into practice, and in so doing, He altered the course of human history with twelve ordinary men who gave up everything to follow *"the Christ, the Son of the living God"* (Matthew 16:16). He led them out of obscurity, away from torn fishing nets and an old boat in need of repair, to live lives worthy of their calling. Not a particularly impressive group by today's

---

[49] Kevin Mercer, D.J. Burns thanks God as N.C. State makes improbable Sweet 16 run in NCAA Tournament, *Sports Spectrum,* Mar 25, 2024, retrieved from https://sportsspectrum.com/sport/basketball/2024/03/25/dj-burns-thanks-god-nc-state-ncaa-tournament/.

standards, but they learned how to live and how to make their lives count for eternity. They were never seen the same again.

Jesus understood the historical record, the wisdom literature of the Old Testament, the Torah, and the words of the prophets, all of which were at the heart of His life. Certainly, the Bible must hold the same place in our own lives. We might find ourselves with fewer headaches, a whole lot less insecurity, and a clearer view of where we are going and how to get there. Jesus knew the contents of the Scriptures—its stories, its instructions, its laws and statutes, its value, and its purpose. Every decision Jesus ever made, every significant event, every move, every turn in the road during His 33 years, was guided by His Father's words. No exceptions. Every day was the same—God's word was central and critical for His earthly life, but it also carried supernatural ramifications for the life to come. We can expect no less from a life lived well to the glory of God and centered in the word and will of God.

In his award-winning book *Knowing God's Truth*, author Jon Nielson stated his take on the importance of thoughtful and careful study of the Scriptures.

> God is not silent. He has not left us guessing about what He wants. But we must actively study His Word…The most basic reason why the study of biblical theology is important is that it is about God; it is the study of our Creator, Savior, and King…What we believe about God has an impact on the choices we make—even the small ones—every single day…God, in His Word, reveals to us the deepest realities about our world: His role in creation, the sinfulness of humanity, His sovereign purpose and plan, and the salvation that is available only through Christ Jesus, His Son. Careful (study of

the Bible), then, matters because it is a way for us to understand and make sense of the world.[50]

The late Christian scholar, G. Ernest Wright, wrote in the opening words of his commentary, *Book of the Acts of God: An Introduction to the Bible*:

> Christianity has always held that the Bible is a very special book, unlike any other book in the world. It is the most important of all books because in it, and in it alone, the true God has made Himself known to man with clarity. The world is full of sacred literature, and it is full of gods. But in the vast confusion the one source that can be relied upon for truth is the Bible.
>
> There we are told about events which brought the church into being, and the purpose for its being. There we encounter the answer to the meaning of our lives and of the history in which we live. There the frightening gulf between our weak, ignorant and mortal lives and the infinity of power and space is really bridged. There, we discover our duty defined and our God revealed.[51]

Most of us don't realize or fully appreciate what we've got in our hands, the book of the ages, where

> **Hebrews 4:12, MSG** - *God means what he says. What he says goes. His powerful Word is sharp as a surgeon's scalpel, cutting through everything...*

---

[50] Jon Nielson, A God who speaks, *Christianity Today*, January/February 2024, 40-41
[51] Reginald Horace Fuller and G. Ernest Wright, *Book of the Acts of God: An Introduction to the Bible,* (Doubleday, 1957), 13.

> *laying us open to listen and obey. Nothing and no one can resist God's Word. We can't get away from it—no matter what.*

This is not just another book, and it should not ever be treated as such. It has stood the test of time, relentless scrutiny, criticism, and challenge like no other publication for generations. Yet it stands undaunted and sure. Kings and kingdoms come and go, but the Bible remains *"the living and enduring word of God"* (1 Peter 1:23. NIV). Again, John MacArthur reminds us:

> We believe in the Word of God. We believe that it is inspired. We believe that it is without error in the original autographs, and God has protected and preserved it to this day so that it substantially remains faithful to its original revelation. We believe that when the Word speaks, we are commanded to listen. That's why the Bible is the theme of everything we do. We define life [values & priorities, love, marriage, the family, etc.] and ministry in biblical terms. It is what we believe, it is how we behave, and it is the message we proclaim. And the Bible claims to be the very Word of God and it does so in an unaffected and unambiguous way…[52]

Scholars are not sure who wrote it, but Psalm 119 sums up the reality and benefit of making God's word and law *"the joy of (one's) heart"* (v. 111). Simply, it brings results, God's best— wisdom, understanding, insight, divine instruction, guidance, strength and courage (Psalm 119:97-104). It is a *"lamp to my feet, and a light to my path"* (v.105), keeping me centered and on the right road. *"The*

---

[52] John MacArthur, Assorted attacks on the Bible, *Grace to You*, 2024, retrieved from https://www.gty.org/library/sermons-library/90-320/assorted-attacks-on-the-bible.

very essence of God's word is truth." (Psalm 119:160), and truth frees us to be the men and/or women God wants us to be, free of uncertainty, vain pursuits, and poor decisions.

Psalm 97:105 (MSG) –

I watch my step, avoiding the ditches and ruts of evil so I can spend all my time keeping your Word.
I never make detours from the route you laid out;
you gave me such good directions...
With your instruction, I understand life...
By your words I can see where I'm going...

An absolute necessity.

Martin Luther (1483-1546) understood the place and power of the Word of God in facing everyday life and encountering the reality of evil. He wrote, *A Mighty Fortress Is Our God* in 1529. It was my ordination hymn.

The Prince of Darkness grim, we tremble not for him;
His rage we can endure, for lo, his doom is sure,
One little word shall fell him...
That word above all earthly pow'rs...
God's truth abideth still,
His kingdom is forever[53].

Under orders from God, Moses reluctantly showed up in Pharaoh's palace to demand that he set Israel free after four hundred years of slavery. He began with these words: *"Thus says the Lord, the God (Yahweh), the God (Elohim) of Israel"* (Exodus 5:1). Egypt was unimpressed, but that would soon change. They countered with, *"Thus says Pharaoh"* (Exodus 5:9), and a war of competing ideas, ideologies, and worldviews was on for the supremacy and control of

---

[53] Martin Luther, *A Mighty Fortress Is Our God*, Public Domain, 1529.

men and women everywhere. *"Thus says the Lord"* or *"Thus says Pharaoh."* Make your choice. A battle of words has raged again and again throughout the centuries in the minds and hearts of us all.

God spoke with directness and power through His servant Moses. His word and will were made plain. This was not a proposal. No negotiations. These were orders. His commands are not recommendations, nor are they optional. They never are—not for Pharaoh and Egypt, and certainly not for us.

God had spoken with authority, and there was no mistaking what He wanted: *"Let My people go* (imperative)...*"* (Exodus 5:1-20)—liberty to live free of enslavement, as God intended. Nothing else really mattered. If we want to experience the very best God has to offer, God's will is always to be obeyed. It's that simple. Pharaoh and the rest of us would do well to comply with divine orders and law. No exceptions tolerated. No excuses accepted. Grab your Bible. Know what it says. Do what it tells you. Moses did. Jesus did. You and I can do no less.

In short, the knowledge, application, and injection of bibliocentric life essentials into daily living makes possible a life that will mightily influence your little corner of the world for the better. It straightens out my thinking, clarifies my personal values, shows me what to avoid, and what I must do. God's word directs us to God Himself "and keeps us anchored in ageless truth... (and) connects us with our past and points us to our future[54] "—something Pharaoh never learned, and in the end, it cost him plenty. In the introduction of his book *Growing Deep in the Christian Life*, Charles Swindoll remarked:

---

[54] Peter Dehaan, Ten Reasons Why the bible is important, Pursuing Biblical Christianity, 2024, retrieved from

> The need for knowledge of the Scripture is obvious. Everywhere I turn, I meet or hear about well-meaning Christians who are long on zeal but short on facts… lots of enthusiasm and motivation but foggy when it comes to scriptural truth.
>
> They have a deep and genuine desire to be used by God, to reach the lost, to serve in the church, to invest their energies in "the kingdom of God and His righteousness," but their doctrinal foundation is shifting sand rather than solid rock. The result is predictable: They are at the mercy of their emotions, flying high one day and scraping the bottom the next. A frustrating 'yo-yo syndrome.[55]

Standing on the banks of the Red Sea, the people suffered from the "yo-yo syndrome," up one moment, excited about God's intervention in liberating them from slavery, and down in the next, wondering if they wouldn't have been better off staying in Egypt. But the word of the living God was about to be released, and the people were about to witness the power of His word to rescue and save. The waters opened, just as God said they would, allowing Israel to pass through on dry ground and escape the sword and spear of Egypt. His word moved a frightened, anxious people forward. There was really no other choice in the matter: follow God's instructions and live, or surrender to Pharaoh's rule and die. There has always been but one choice, a choice we all must make at one point or another—life or death, blessing or curse, His way or my way, compliance or defiance. Take your pick. Do as God said and walk free, or stay and feel the point of Egypt's vengeance. His word is for our benefit.

---

[55] Charles Swindoll, *Growing Deep in the Christian Life*, (

Pharaoh ignored God's sovereignty, and it cost him dearly—the heart of a nation, the life of his firstborn at Passover, and the total annihilation of his army. They were all lost—a high price to pay for arrogance and rebellion. Every soldier died in the waters of the Red Sea, just as God said. Pharaoh lived and died at the mercy of his own moral failure and stubbornness. Moses, on the other hand, went on to live a life that mattered. There is a lesson here to be learned.

The scrolls of the Old and New Testaments record the teachings and events that formed the foundation upon which Jesus lived a life that mattered. He never wavered or strayed from the eternal word of God, His Father. He stayed the course laid out for Him in the throne room of heaven, where God so ordered redemption's plan and story. Jesus never deviated from His role as God's favorite Son, the Savior of the world, the sacrificial Lamb of God who would shed His blood for the forgiveness of humanity's sin. His faith and trust in His Father's word never failed Him, even as a Roman spear pierced His flesh and He suffered unmercifully on a cross until His breath was no more. He stayed true to the end. So should we. God's word will not fail us... ever.

He was then placed in a borrowed tomb, and there He remained, but not for long. *"He was buried, and he was raised from the dead on the third day, just as the Scriptures said"* (1 Corinthians 15:4, NLT). Note the last five words of that verse—*"just as the Scriptures said."* They are critical. *The Son of Man* would rise and conquer the grave, *"just as the Scriptures said"* (Luke 18:31-34). God always does what He says He will do. Count on it. Do life God's way, and you will always get God's results. Resurrection. New life. New plan and purpose, a life that matters.

For a few moments, all seemed lost in the shadow of the cross and a dark tomb. Spiritual blindness is a real thing—the inability to see what God is doing in the toughest of days. It happened to

Jeremiah and God's people, who needed to know that God had other plans in place—better plans beyond anything they could have ever thought or imagined. God sent word in the form of a *"letter,"* postmarked from Jerusalem to a people trying to make life work in a pagan Babylon. Sounds familiar, doesn't it? God's word was, and is, designed to bring much-needed encouragement, comfort, and stability to its recipients, those dragged off into captivity and facing a world without promise or dreams. God sent the following word: *"I know what I'm doing. I have it all planned out—plans to take care of you, not abandon you, plans to give you the future you hope for"* (Jeremiah 29:1, MSG).

God had a plan for a young man I knew. His name was Daniel. Let me tell you his story.

I met Daniel a good number of years ago. Little did I know at the time that he was a troubled teen with a past filled with moral failures, disappointments, poor decisions, and worse behavior.

He said, "The teachers hated me." He was always in trouble, but blessed with extraordinary athleticism. He excelled at sports, particularly soccer, which became his god. Soccer was the means he used to find approval and gain acceptance and fulfillment. He eventually was offered an athletic scholarship to play collegiately, an opportunity few receive. The providence of God brought him to a Christian college where I was coaching.

He told me later that during his high school days, he began to drink heavily, following in the footsteps of other family members.

> *"Drinking,"* he said, *became a regular thing in my life along with the parties, the people, the girls and the experiences that go along with all these things. I'd take it all back in a heartbeat; I wish I knew back*

> *then what I know now. My heart bleeds for the people I wronged"*

He watched as one of his close friends, only 19 years old, was beaten to death at a party. On another occasion, while out partying, he saw his then-soccer coach punch his best friend and throw him down a flight of stairs.

He writes,

> *"My life was in a downward spiral, and I had no way to come out of it on my own. I can remember one night looking at my life and seeing some very close similarities to both my alcoholic uncles. I remember becoming emotional and angry and just wishing for a way out; I don't think that I was praying by any means, but I know that Jesus was listening and had much bigger plans for my life... I believe that God brought me to Bryan College and surrounded me with amazing people to show me that there is a better life to be had."*

The transition did not come easy for Daniel. He struggled in this new Christian environment, which, admittedly, he didn't understand. He knew nothing of Christ or the gospel. He was disillusioned and frustrated. He wanted out. He wanted to run—get away, anywhere—but God would not let him go. He had plans for His son.

Several years later, just before his senior year, my assistant coach and I sent him to the California Seahorses to play soccer for the summer, and I started to pray. The Seahorses are a team with a Christian emphasis and ministry focus, utilizing soccer as a platform for the Gospel to reach young people with the message of the cross and God's love.

Before the summer ended, Daniel wrote me a letter. He told me of how God put other young men, his teammates, into his life who had similar problems, who were honest and open, and who struggled with the same things Daniel did, but they had found the answer... and it was Christ. He wrote, *"I get it now. I've committed my life to Christ, and I'm reading the Bible and can't get enough of it."* That was significant. I knew straight away that a change had taken place. He returned to college later that fall... and then I saw it. The old man was gone. The slate had been wiped clean—a new man had emerged, a new *"creation"* had risen from the ashes of despair and defeat. A once lost, broken, bitter young man, with no path forward and no future to speak of, was found by the grace of God and captured by the message of God's love and the word of the living God, who gives life to the dead. Daniel was made whole, *"born of the Spirit"* (John 3:8). God's word did its work and transformed him *"by the renewing of his mind"* (Romans 12:2), and raised him up with a new found purpose for living. With God's truth now pulsating through his veins, he was full of joy, hope, and the promise of finally being able to live a life that matters. God rescued his soul, *"according to His mercy, by the washing of regeneration and renewing by the Holy Spirit"* (Titus 3:5).

Later that fall, we took Daniel up to Pocket Wilderness. There, he stood before his teammates, gave his testimony, and told them of his journey from death to life. That afternoon, we baptized him in the cool mountain waters of Tennessee.

Some years later, following graduation, he wrote me again,

> *"My life has changed so much since I committed my life to Him (Christ)... I live life with a lot more joy now and see things through much different lenses. I have felt God pulling on my heart for a while now to go into ministry and be a shepherd (a pastor), a*

> *fisher of men to call those who are lost closer to Him... I am very much looking forward to this journey... I am listening for his call, and am ready as His servant."*

A remarkable, miraculous transformation. Daniel went on to seminary, studied the Word of God, and today he serves the cause of Christ as the pastor of a local church, making a difference in the world.

From the cradle to the grave, Jesus was immersed in the knowledge of God's word. From His mother, Mary, He learned, *"With God, nothing is ever impossible, and no word from God shall be without power or impossible of fulfillment"* (Luke 1:37, AMPC). From Joseph, His earthly father, He learned, *"God (is) with us"* in the ups and downs of daily living (Matthew 1:23). Jesus lived, died, and rose from the dead in the power of the Spirit of God and under the direction of His heavenly Father. The life of Christ was no surprise to Him or to the *"many angels encircling the throne... myriads of myriads and thousands of thousands, crying in a great voice, 'Worthy is the Lamb who was slain to receive power and riches and wisdom, and strength and honor and glory and blessing'"* (Revelation 5:11-12, PHILLIPS). Jesus lived and died like it mattered, and all eternity knew it. He lived focused, deliberate, steady, empowered. His life and death, every word He uttered, the roads He traveled, the people He met along the way—every bit of it counted. That's for me.

One Sunday morning, I met eighty-year-old Richard Floyd in the hallway of his home church in Chattanooga. We talked for about twenty minutes about his life, the grace and mercy of God, the cross of Christ, and where God had taken him. Richard is a former member of the Tennessee State General Assembly, where he served from 2006 to 2014.

He told me about the day he retired from his post in Nashville. I could see the tears well up in his eyes as he recalled those final moments. He was invited by the Speaker to share a few parting words with his colleagues. He quickly and somewhat reluctantly accepted the opportunity and honor, and walked to the podium, praying every step of the way, asking God to speak through him. He didn't know what to say. He had not prepared a speech. He stood at the podium, looked out over a room full of politicians (a tough crowd), and spoke from his heart. At that moment, Richard was no longer a politician. He said, "I'm not the sharpest knife in the drawer (I can relate to that). But what I do know, I know real good." Then he lifted his Bible, which was always with him, high above his head. "This is what I know," he declared. "Jesus loves me, this I know, for the Bible—this book right here—tells me so," and then he sat down.

The Sunday school chorus I sang as a kid many years ago is still relevant and true, especially in today's world:

The B-I-B-L-E,
Yes, that's the book for me!
I stand alone on the Word of God,
the B-I-B-L-E![56]

The message is clear. There is nothing more important (except maybe the Author of the Book) for those who want to live decisively and Christianly in a world that has gone absolutely mad. There is no other way to live that makes sense or that truly matters. The centrality of God's word in my life must remain. It is how Jesus lived. It is how we must live.

The British evangelist Smith Wigglesworth (1859-1947) was instrumental in the Pentecostal movement of a hundred years ago.

---

[56] Anonymous, Public Domain, retrieved from https://hymnary.org/text/the_b_i_b_l_e_yes_thats_the_book.

He was often referred to as the "Apostle of Faith." He said of the Scriptures:

> The Bible is the Word of God: supernatural in origin, eternal in duration, inexpressible in valor, infinite in scope, regenerative in power, infallible in authority, universal in interest, personal in application, inspired in totality. Read it through, write it down, pray it in, work it out, and then pass it on. Truly, it is the Word of God. It brings into man the personality of God; it changes the man until he becomes the epistle of God. It transforms his mind, changes his character, takes him on from grace to grace, and gives him an inheritance in the Spirit. God comes in, dwells in, walks in, talks through, and sups with him.[57]

In April of 1521, Martin Luther was called before Charles V to "recant and revoke" what he had written regarding his position on justification by faith and Rome's muddled theology, practice, and leadership.[58] He stood before the council at Worms with uncommon boldness, great conviction, and raw courage. He declared for all to hear.

> "My conscience is so bound and held captive by these Scriptures...
> I will not and may not revoke any manner of thing...
> I don't have anything else to say...I am tied by the Scriptures."[59]

---

[57] Craig T. Owens, 17 quotes from "Smith Wigglesworth On Prayer, Power, And Miracles," Post. January 15, 2014, retrieved from https://craigtowens.com/2014/01/15/17-quotes-from-smith-wigglesworth-on-prayer-power-and-miracles/.
[58] John Foxe (rewritten by Harold J. Chadwick), *The New Foxe's Book of Martyrs 2001*, (Gainesville, Florida" Bridge-Logos, 2001), 147-149.
[59] Ibid, 150.

Little did he know that his words would echo down the corridors of church history and through the halls of eternity. There was no doubt about the blueprint for Luther's daily affairs and the foundation upon which he would build the years and ministry before him. His life mattered, and the fires of the great Reformation were lit by a lone monk who took God's word seriously—his mind, his heart, his actions "tied by the Scriptures." Life must be lived no other way. A life that matters is only built upon the foundation of the Word of the Living God.

"None of us got where we are solely by pulling ourselves up by our bootstraps. We got here because somebody – a parent, a teacher, an Ivy League crony or a few nuns – bent down and helped us pick up our boots."[60]

— Thurgood Marshall,
U.S. Supreme Court Justice

---

[60] Editors, 9 Powerful Quotes by Thurgood Marshall, *Biography*, January 28, 2021, retrieved from https://www.biography.com/legal-figures/thurgood-marshall-quotes.

CHAPTER 4

ENGAGE THE WORLD.

John 4:1-10, MSG - *"...So Jesus left the Judean countryside and went back to Galilee.*

To get there, he had to pass through Samaria. He came into Sychar, a Samaritan village...Jacob's well was still there...It was noon.

A woman, a Samaritan, came to draw water. Jesus said, "Would you give me a drink of water?"...

The Samaritan woman, taken aback, asked, "How come you, a Jew, are asking me, a Samaritan woman, for a drink?" (Jews in those days wouldn't be caught dead talking to Samaritans.)

Jesus answered, "If you knew the generosity of God and who I am, you would be asking me for a drink, and I would give you fresh, living water"

Years ago, a young man getting ready to graduate from college asked me the following question: "What does God want me to do with my life?" A serious question every follower of Christ must ask. I quickly responded, "Get your hands dirty. Invest in people and their lives because that's what Jesus did. You do the same. It's the only way to go."

Engage the world. Leave the hallowed halls of the church and the confines of our self-made monasteries. Get yourself out there, where men and women live and die, work, play, and encounter untold hardships, unspeakable misery, disappointments, and all manner of trouble. Deliberately put yourself in the thick of it, where people succeed and fail, trying to survive destructive patterns of living that *"steal and kill and destroy"* (John 10:10). Deliver hope *"in the name of Jesus"* in those dark places, bringing the love, mercy, forgiveness, and healing power of God to bear on the lives of those struggling to make it through another day. In short, to engage the world is to tear down the kingdom of darkness where Satan rules and raise up the standard of the kingdom of God, where Christ is King. That matters because people's lives matter greatly.

As a young girl, Saint Teresa of Avila (1515-1582), a Carmelite nun, gave what little money she had to the poor. She was "resolved to do a kind action or say a kind word to everyone she met… [bringing] sunshine with her wherever she went." Wholly given over to God, she engaged her world, living daily on the lookout for opportunities to minister the love and mercy of God. She loved the sick, and the sick loved her.[61] She wrote,

> Christ has no body but yours,
> No hands, no feet on earth but yours,

---

[61] Jennie Chappell, William Bramwell, and A. T.. Pierson, *25 Classic Christian Women Biographies: Timeless Classics That Will Strengthen and Inspire*, (Classic Christin Ebooks, Kindle Edition), 533.

Yours are the eyes with which He looks
Compassion on this world,
Yours are the feet with which He walks to do good,
Yours are the hands with which He blesses all the world.
Yours are the hands, yours are the feet,
Yours are the eyes, you are His body.
Christ has no body now but yours,
No hands, no feet on earth but yours,
Yours are the eyes with which He looks
Compassion on this world.
Christ has no body now on earth but yours.[62]

A great perspective for every believer wanting to make his or her life count for the Kingdom of God.

Shortly after Pentecost, when the Holy Spirit fell upon the disciples of Christ, Peter and John were on their way to the Temple. They encountered a lame man on the streets of Jerusalem begging for help. They stopped and said, *"I don't have any money for you. But I will give you what I have. In the name of Jesus Christ of Nazareth, get up and walk"* (Acts 3:1-7). Those words changed the man's life forever. The future ministry of the church was set at the very beginning of its birth: Help people to their feet. Help people move forward. Do what you can with what you've got—the power and love of God—to make a difference in the world, to live like it matters… because it does. It certainly did for that poor, broken man and for the two followers of Christ, who probably left the Temple feeling good about themselves and their newfound ministry.

In 1911, British journalist and writer Holbrook Jackson (1874-1948) published a book entitled *Platitudes in the Making*, a

---

[62]Teresa of Avila, Christ has no body, *Journey with Jesus*, retrieved from https://www.journeywithjesus.net/poemsandprayers/3637-Teresa_Of_Avila_Christ_Has_No_Body.

collection of short, pithy statements reflecting an approach to life in the early 1900s. Jackson sent a copy of his book to G.K. Chesterton, who immediately challenged Jackson's ideas. Jackson wrote, "Don't think—(just) Do." Chesterton countered, "Do think—(then) Do!"[63] Wise counsel. Take note. Chesterton's words apply to living life like it matters in a world that needs help. Engage the culture with the truth of the gospel message. Pray a good deal. Think first, then do… and in that order—pray, think, act.

Philip W. Eaton, the ninth president (1995-2012) of Seattle Pacific University, warned that as Christians, we cannot narrow our influence in the world.

> We must learn a new language, a new posture of fearlessness, a new posture of winsomeness. We must focus outward, always seeking to engage the culture and change the world with our story (the story of what is true and good and beautiful, our ancient Christian story)—never yielding to the comfort and security of withdrawal or separatism, either Christian or intellectual. We must commit to being in the mix, on the leading edge of our culture and the cultures of the world, always seeking to be relevant, to be helpful, to be responsive to the needs of the communities we serve and the world we hope to impact for good.[64]

Something we have not always been willing to do. The need for the church to think biblically first, and then do as Jesus would do, is

---

[63] Trevin Wax, *Orthodoxy: With Annotations and Guided Readings by Trevin Wax*, (Nashville, Tennessee: B&H Academics, 2022) x.
[64] Philip W. Eaton, *Engaging the Culture, Changing the World*, (Downers Grove, IL: Intervarsity Press, 2011), 8, 28.

what every believer should strive for—a willingness to engage people right where they live, right where they are.

I knew a wonderful man, a former college professor and pastor, who was dying of pancreatic cancer. The disease had sapped his energy. He lost weight at an alarming rate, was in pain much of the time, and what little strength he had left was quickly fading. The doctors gave him just five weeks to live. But none of it stopped him. He continued his ministry despite his setbacks. He was one tough guy with a big heart who loved people and loved God. His tenacity for ministry was other-worldly. He managed to get himself out of bed, got dressed with some help, and then got a ride to visit an eighty-year-old man who was bedridden and struggling physically. He had been hospitalized at a local rehab center for weeks, trying to recover his failing strength. The mission was simple: bring communion, celebrate together the cross, the resurrection of Christ, their own redemption, and their relationship with God and each other. It was beautiful and sacred, an encouragement for both to "keep on keeping on." Such an unselfish, compassionate act of love and kindness. He engaged his culture and brought the love of Christ to a hurting man, and that mattered. He mattered, and it mattered to his friend. He made a difference in the world.

Engaging the culture is about helping people when they need it most. It means stepping in with a cup of cold water when you see the need, or offering a hand to lift someone out of the muck and mire of poor choices and questionable behavior that often end in destroyed lives and broken hearts. There is no place for harsh criticism and condemnation (more on that in a moment) when taking on the pain of others who have either caught a bad break or failed miserably in their personal lives. Learning to walk in the moccasins of others helps in that process. Connecting with people is about presenting with clarity, surety, empathy, and kindness—an alternative approach to daily living than what is currently practiced, an option that is more positive, more productive, more constructive, more safe, more loving, and more in line with the God of the Scriptures, who "loves people more than anything else,"[65] and knows what it takes to live like it matters. Moving to the frontlines of the battle for the minds and hearts of all manner of men and women is about rescue and restoration, getting people back up on their feet, dusting them off, and setting those who have lost their way on a new path that leads to a life that truly matters for them and for yourself.

Darryl Strawberry, whose number "18" was retired by the NY Mets, called Jesus the "Miracle Maker," for the radical change that took place in his life, rescuing and redeeming him to live fully and purposefully beyond the baseball diamond.[66] Wasted years behind him—the alcohol, drugs, an abusive father, divorce, colon cancer, the rehab centers, and more—this Baseball Hall of Famer is now living a life that matters, committed to Christ and His kingdom. He, along with his wife, Tracy, started a foundation to help children struggling with autism. When Darryl had a heart attack at age sixty-two, he said, "Every day I'm off the road is one less person I could help." Darryl Strawberry has engaged his world, and that matters.

Jesus said, *"I came that they may have and enjoy life, and have it in abundance (to the full, till it overflows)"* (John 10:10, AMPC). That's the goal, and it should be ours as we represent God in Christ in the world in which we live. That's the objective. That is what God desires from followers of Christ—to connect with the world in a meaningful way. Jesus was the greatest social worker who ever lived. No doubt, we can do better than we have and must do better, investing in people.

---

[65] A phrase my pastor, Gary Jared, repeats often.
[66] Video interview, Darryl Strawberry's greatest gift to God, *Christian Broadcasting Network*, July 8 2024, retrieved from https://www2.cbn.com/video/stories/darryl-strawberrys-greatest-gift-god.

Anthony Brown was driving across a bridge over Interstate 40 when he spotted a stranger in distress. The man was standing on the bridge, ready to jump to his death and end his pain. Brown said, "My first thought was I needed to help him, because we are here to love and care for one another on this earth." Having already lost his brother to suicide, Brown was not about to ignore this troubled man. He stopped and approached him.

Initially, the distressed man "claimed there was nothing Brown could do to help him." Brown said, "I let him know that I was not there to judge him and that I cared for him. I also told him about my brother who committed suicide. He was shocked that a stranger would stop and care about his well-being." The man responded and stepped away from the edge of the bridge. A tragedy was avoided, a life was saved, because one man, full of compassion, was concerned enough to engage a stranger and meet him at the point of his need. Brown said, "If I were to meet [the distressed man] again, I would tell him that it is not his time to die yet, that God has bigger plans for him."[67]

Brown invested in that man's life—a stranger, disheartened, discouraged, hopeless, and alone. Brown did not know him. He had no knowledge of his background, where he had been in life, anything about his prior relationships, his status, or his losses. All he knew was that this man was in trouble, suffering, hurting, and needing help. He chose to get involved. Good choice. He allowed himself to feel and then acted to rescue and redeem. That is how Jesus lived. That is how He loved.

---

[67] Louise Bevan, "Passerby Talks Suicidal Man Down From Edge of Bridge: 'I Wasn't There to Judge Him'," *Epoch Times*, (3-29-21).

Jesus hung out with a variety of people from all walks of life, from every socioeconomic background and social standing. He rubbed shoulders with them all—He lived with them, ate with them, listened to them, loved them, and understood them, their dreams, their hopes, their successes, and their failures. He cared for the sick and the dying, the helpless, the hopeless, and the hapless. He fed multitudes who were hungry. He healed the brokenhearted and dined with a hated tax man by the name of Zacchaeus. He even went fishing with a rough bunch of common, blue-collar laborers whose hands were calloused from hard work. No one was rejected or ignored. He loved them all.

He loved children and touched their lives. He healed the daughter of Jairus, a ruler in the synagogue (Mark 5:21-24), a place where Christ was not always welcomed. He healed ten lepers and changed their lives for the better, though only one returned to give thanks. Jesus ran to the home of a Roman centurion, a hardened soldier, a man who was always ready for a fight and accustomed to killing at the command of his superiors. The man begged for help—his daughter was dying—and Jesus showed up for the fight. He healed that little girl. He never looked the other way, but moved with compassion and strength to make life better for anyone in need of divine assistance.

Every day, He interacted with the destitute of this world, —the blind and the lame. He rubbed shoulders with prostitutes and restored their dignity. He made friends with beggars, social outcasts, and street people rejected by society. He wept over the city of Jerusalem for the pain and judgment He knew was coming (Luke 19:41, ESV). He made inroads with the in-crowd and the social elite. No one was excluded, not even the temple money changers who took advantage of their fellow man for profit (John 2:14-17). He confronted their behavior, challenged their ethics, and administered corrective measures to protect the innocent and less fortunate. He got tough when necessary and dealt with the takers and users, the slick politicians, and the religious leaders who hated Him for His popularity and convictions. He got into trouble because He loved them all, even the crowd who called for His death and the soldiers who mocked Him and pounded the nails into His flesh—each one the recipient of His great love, grace, compassion, forgiveness, and mercy. Jesus knew how to engage the culture. He never withdrew from the world; He lived in it. He pressed in, got up close and personal, and brought the truth of God's love into the troubled lives of people.

The one thing Jesus did not do, however, was judge and/or condemn any of them. That was not His mission, and neither is it yours or mine. He told us that He did not come to expose our shortcomings and faults. He neither ridiculed nor set out to embarrass or reveal my flaws and failures, especially with the intent to publicly shame or destroy my reputation. I can do that all by myself. Instead, He made room for my many imperfections and human weaknesses (and I have plenty of both). He loves me right where I am, enough to challenge me to *"follow"* Him and to trust Him as if my very life depended on it... and it does. *"For God did not send the Son into the world in order to judge (to reject, to condemn, to pass sentence on) the world, but that the world might find salvation and be made safe and sound through Him"* (John 3:17, AMPC). That was the goal, and it has been that way from eternity and beyond. Change the world with God's love, always with love, kindness, and mercy from above—the core and heart of Christ. Give people a new spin on life. We desperately need it, all of us. Everywhere Christ went, He brought the hope that things could be better. He came into the world with a simple but profound message: *"God is love"* (1 John 4:8). A new kingdom was coming. A new King had arrived, and life would be different and better than it had ever been before. There is hope for all humanity, and it doesn't rest in a government party, political pundits, religious leaders, church programs, social agendas, the latest fad, designer clothes, or human skills and abilities. Real hope for a better world is centered in Jesus and no one else.

Engage the culture with the person and claims of Christ in your little corner of the world, and your life and mine will matter to the people you rub shoulders with every day. Your spiritual well-being will be healthier, your emotions will be more stable, and the future will look brighter. Your life will be more productive, purposeful, meaningful, and powerful. You will effect change for the better.

In the opening scene of the movie *Gladiator* (one of my favorites), Maximus, the powerful Roman general who was later sold into slavery to fight in the arena, gathered his troops before going into battle against the barbaric tribes of Germania. He shouted, "What you do in life will echo in eternity."[68] A powerful reminder for soldiers going to war, but an even better reminder for followers of Christ who want to make a difference in the world and are willing to leave the safe confines of the church and march out into the community to battle the hordes of hell for the souls and well-being of fallen, desperate men and women. The outcome of that fight will indeed "echo in eternity."

Christian life principles, applied over the long haul to contemporary problems and social ills, will make a difference in your life and on the street where you live. The willingness to "get in the game" is paramount to living like it matters—to show up (that's half the battle) and bring a little bit of Jesus into a world struggling to find its way forward, a world that has lost its moral bearings, a world riddled with destructive life patterns and dominated by an approach to life (daily choices and actions) that is typically void of

---

[68] David Franzon, *Gladiator*, DreamWorks Pictures, Universal Pictures, May 1, 2000.

God and hope for a better tomorrow. The world abounds with alcoholism, drug dealers and users, sex traffickers, pornography, racism, hatred, *"wars and rumors of wars"* (Matthew 24:6), divorce, abandoned and abused children, all manner of sickness, depression, discouragement, sorrows, broken hearts, and much more. The toll in human misery and ruined lives cannot be overestimated. Our world, my world, my neighborhood, school, work, home, and marriage—every bit of it—needs redeeming. Choosing to live like it matters, like Jesus, will get the job done.

Some years ago, American sociologist and Baptist pastor Tony Campolo was working as a junior high summer camp counselor. He noted that kids that age often think having a good time means picking on people, particularly their peers. They are good at finding weaknesses and pointing out flaws without mercy; they have sharp tongues. There was a boy named Billy who suffered from cerebral palsy. His speech was slurred, his body uncoordinated, and he walked and talked with a great deal of difficulty. His fellow campers were cruel and heartless, constantly poking fun at him.

Billy's cabin was assigned the task of leading camp devotions at mid-week. Billy was chosen by the others to take the lead. The intent of the group was to put him up front before the crowd to humiliate, dishonor, and completely devalue him as a person. They were not the least bit interested in hearing what God may say through him. Billy was required to stand before the entire camp, open the Bible and read it aloud, and share with the group the devotional material he had prepared. A tough assignment for any boy, let alone one with his limitations. But he took the challenge. A brave young man.

Billy dragged himself to the front the best he could, stood before his peers, and began to speak. He stammered and slurred his words. The clarity of his speech was poor. His peers laughed, as expected, but he spoke anyway. Campolo said it took Billy five agonizing minutes to get his message out, "Jesus…loves…me…and…I…love…Jesus." When he finished, he agonizingly made his way back to his seat and quietly sat down. Mission accomplished. The entire camp went silent. No one spoke. No one moved. Revival broke out among those kids. Out of that church camp came several who were later called to the mission field and to the pastoral ministry—because a young boy, crippled with debilitating cerebral palsy, who could barely get one foot in front of the other, whose mouth could hardly form the words that told the story of God's love. A remarkable, extraordinary courage to stand up for Christ and engage an antagonistic, hostile culture that preyed on the weak, and ridiculed and mocked the boy's very existence. That young man's life mattered. He made a difference. He was out to change His world, and by the grace of God and some good old fashioned guts, he did just that. Nobody is laughing now.[69] What we do in life will indeed echo in eternity.

The importance of engaging this and future generations with the person and claims of Christ and His gospel cannot be overstated. It is critical to the mission and ministry of every believer, hoping to get in on the action of representing God in Christ in my corner of the world.

I need to pray.

Hear me, O God.
Lord, let me leave no doubt as to where I stand and where my loyalties lie—fully committed to You and Your kingdom. Help me to live an authentic Christian life and show forth clearly, for all heaven and earth to see, the love and mercy of God in Christ Jesus radiating

---

[69] Tony Campolo, Just a Kid with Cerebral Palsy, *Stories for the Heart,* compiled by Alice Gray, (Sisters, Oregon: Multnomah, 1996), 60-61.

in and through me. Help me to live as a "light" set on a hill (Matthew 5:14-16) for every man or woman I engage and interact with this day and the next—my spouse, children, grandchildren, and my neighbors, including the man at the local supermarket stocking shelves, the mother standing on a street corner begging for a little help to feed her kids, the bank teller on her feet all day, and the construction worker covered in dust and dirt. Let me shine forth the glory and mercy of God everywhere my foot steps.

Let me take up spiritual weapons for a spiritual war, and fight the good fight of faith with the truth of God's word. Get me in the battle for the souls and the healing of hurting, broken people, and the advancement of Your kingdom. May I gain a good reputation in heaven among the saints and angels. More importantly, may I gain a fearful reputation in Hell and shake the very foundations of evil with the choices I make every day to get involved in the lives of people. Let the world see that I am truly and intimately connected to You, O God—that every success, every good deed, every kind word is due to Your holy presence in me, finding expression in the mundane affairs of daily living. May my life be so real, so genuine, and so true, especially in a world that knows so little of such things. Be Jesus in me, that I might be Jesus to others and thereby make a difference in their lives and on the street where I live.

Lord, let it be so in me. Amen.

Engage the world in the name of Christ. Don't wait. Bend down, and help people put their *"boots"* on. It will revolutionize your life.

"When heaven is about to confer a great responsibility on any man, it will exercise his mind with suffering, subject his sinews and bones to hard work, expose his body to hunger, put him to poverty, place obstacles in the paths of his deeds, so as to stimulate his mind, harden his nature, and improve wherever he is incompetent."[70]

– **Meng Tzu** *(Mencius) fourth century BC*

---

[70] Greg Lukianoff and Jonathan Haidt, *The Coddling of the American Mind*, (Penguin Books, 2019), 19.

Chapter 5

"WE CAN DO IT IF WE WILL" - THE PURPOSE AND PLAN OF GOD

John 4:34 - *Jesus said to them, "My food (nourishment) is to do the will (pleasure) of Him Who sent Me and to accomplish and completely finish His work" (AMPC).*

John 5:30 - *I do not seek or consult My own will [I have no desire to do what is pleasing to Myself, My own aim, My own purpose] but only the will and pleasure of the Father Who sent Me.*

In December 2015, Tiger Woods was a 39-year-old golf professional, once at the top of his game, but no more. Injuries had sidelined him, along with a string of ten infidelities that cost him his marriage, his family, his reputation, and his peace of mind and heart.

When asked by reporters about his return to action, his response was, "No timetable. That's the hardest part. There's really nothing I can look forward to or nothing to build for. Where is the light at the end of the tunnel?" he asked mournfully. "I am really good at playing video games. (Now there's a productive, purposeful day's work.) "That's basically how I pass a lot of my time."[71] The silence of the crowds that once cheered him on to victory is deafening. He admitted that he was on leave from golf to repair the damage he caused by his moral failure.[72]

Here was a man without a future, with little purpose and an uncertain outlook. Pitifully lost. No career other than that of a has-been. The applause of the crowd and the heights of glory had long since faded. Not much to show for his nearly forty years—a sad commentary. No life of any substance, just a room full of yesterday's trophies, video games, and a Masters' green sport jacket hanging in his closet. Not much to brag about these days—a man who squandered his talent and his time chasing a dream of little consequence and a few moments of fleeting recognition and pleasure. This is what happens when a person lives solely to please himself or herself (cf. John 5:30). Life can be, and must be, better than that. Real purpose and significance are needed for life to be satisfying, for it to count for something beyond "being really good" at *Grand Theft Auto* and *Call of Duty* video games. God made us for a reason, a purpose, and He has a good plan to secure for you a life that truly matters. This is no video game. It's life. There is a bigger picture here than a fifty-inch TV screen and a set of golf clubs.

The focus of Jesus' life remained uncomplicated and straightforward. Every hour of His life belonged to God, His Father. Every day, every moment, without exception. He said, *"For I have come down from heaven not to do My own will and purpose but to do the will and purpose of Him Who sent Me"* (John 6:38, AMPC). Pretty clear. Do likewise.

---

[71] Staff, Tiger Woods: no timetable for comeback – is his career over? *The Week*, December 2, 2015.
[72] Staff, Gossip: Tiger Woods, *The Week*, January 8, 2015.

On another occasion, Jesus said, *"I know where I came from and where I am going... For I always do what pleases Him"* (John 8:14, 29, AMPC). You should, too. The latter part of that statement troubles and challenges me the most—three words, *"always... pleases... Him,"* hit too close to home. They represent an area of personal weakness, especially the word *"always."* I admit I'm not *"always"* about delighting myself in God or pleasing Him unless it serves my purpose. In fact, I am more about pleasing myself, which has often been my first concern. One mission-minded Christian, dedicated to serving the destitute and poor of Costa Rica, observed:

> there is a formidable opponent who rises with us each morning, walks with us each day, and shares our thoughts each evening. He is a thief... a thief who quietly promises purpose, fulfillment, and joy, but all the while is stealing from us. His name is SELF.[73]

I'm all about SELF. Most of us are.

Sometimes I have relegated God to little more than an afterthought, much like Israel, who sought the Lord only when life turned sour and they needed His help to serve their own interests (Judges 6:1-10). Halfhearted commitments and split loyalties, however, to the purpose and plan of God and His kingdom, and serving "me, myself, and I" is simply not going to cut it. There is more…much more.

Mark 12:30, AMPC - *And you shall love the Lord your God out of and with your whole heart and out of and with all your soul (your life) and out of and with all your mind (with your faculty of thought and your moral understanding)*

---

[73] Joey Johnson, Thinking of others before ourselves, Mission Update from Costa Rica, September 17, 2024.

and out of and with all your strength. This is the first and principal commandment.

That standard alone will revolutionize your life—loving the Lord without reservation and committing yourself (me too) to fulfilling His purpose and plans for our lives with everything we've got. Nothing less will do. The Bible exhorts us to *"strip off every weight that slows us down, especially the sin that so easily trips us up. And let us run with endurance the race God has set before us"* (Hebrews 12:1, NLT). Olympian Eric Liddell, who won a gold medal in 1924, spoke of life in general. He said, "In the dust of defeat as well as in the laurel of victory, there is glory to be found if one has done his best."[74] I'm still in pursuit of that ideal—doing my best—and the glory of living a life that truly matters every day.

George Harrison of the Beatles died of cancer at fifty-eight years old. He was the lead guitarist for the Fab Four, a quiet, thoughtful, and pensive man searching for peace, strength, and the answers to the great questions that haunt us all. Harrison stated, "The purpose of life is to find out who am I, why am I here, and where am I going? That's what we need answering."[75] Insightful. He was right on the mark. His final message to the world was enlightening. He often said, "Everything else can wait, but the search for God cannot wait…"[76] Correct on all points. We need to know God now,

---

[74] Jordan Raynor, IF success comes from God THEN inputs are greater than outcomes, May 13, 2024, retrieved from https://www.jordanraynor.com/blog/if-success-comes-from-god-then-inputs-outcomes#:~:text=Christian%20Olympian%20Eric%20Liddell%20once,a%20position%20of%20rest%20today!

[75] Videoholic 2000s, *CBS Evening News – 'On the Death of George Harrison, Nov. 2001,' YouTube* (10-14-09), retrieved from https://www.youtube.com/watch?v=P5gxTJi5KOU&list=PL59AFB55CFABD53F2&index=1.

[76] Billboard Staff, George Harrison Dies At 58, Billboard, Music News, November 30, 2001, retrieved from https://www.billboard.com/music/music-news/george-harrison-dies-at-58-77597/.

and we need to see His plan and purpose activated in our day-to-day lives. It is important. It is vital to our personal well-being.

Jesus knew for certain why He left the palaces of heaven to walk the roads of the ancient world—to heal the sick, raise the dead, speak the truth to all who would listen, climb Golgotha's hill, rise from the dead three days later, and fulfill His Father's purpose for His life. His direction and daily focus were divinely prescribed and outlined from eternity past. From the manger to the grave, His life was set and remained squarely on redemption's plan. It started with the angel's announcement: His name will be Jesus. *"He will be great, and will be called the Son of the Most High, and the Lord God will give Him the throne of His father David... and His kingdom will have no end"* (Luke 1:31-33).

Everything was ordered in that direction. Nothing was missing. Nothing was left to chance. No day was wasted. He did what He was designed to do, what He had been called to do, gifted to do, and ultimately, He took what was rightly His—a seat next to His Father in the throne room of heaven. Christ had come to ensure that God's rescue plan was put into motion. That was His mission, nothing else. It is also my task, my mission, and yours. As Mark Twain said, "The two most important days in your life are the day you were born and the day you discover the reason why."

Jesus walked into the temple at Nazareth and read from the prophet Isaiah:

> **Luke 4:18-19, ESV** – *The Spirit of the Lord is upon me, because he has anointed me to proclaim good news to the poor. He has sent me to proclaim liberty to the captives and recovering of sight to the blind, to set at liberty those who are oppressed, to proclaim the year of the Lord's favor.*

He closed the book, took a seat, and said, *"Today this Scripture has been fulfilled in your hearing"* (Luke 4:21, ESV). And all Hell ran for cover.

At the close of His life, Jesus looked back over His short thirty-three years and concluded with absolute confidence and certainty, *"It is finished"* (John 19:30), a summary statement of the redemptive life He lived. God's purpose and plan for Him were fully fulfilled in His daily life, His death, and His resurrection. He got the job done. I might want those few words carved on my tombstone for having completed God's design for my life. They were His last and final words before death arrived. Redemption secured. The way to the *"tree of life"* (Genesis 3:22; Revelation 22:2) was opened once again. Pain and suffering would one day be no more, and the gates of eternity were swung open for the saints of the ages to walk through triumphantly. Mission accomplished. Right up to the very end, He stayed the course God the Father set for Him, even comforting and encouraging a dying thief: *"Truly, I say to you, today you will be with me in paradise"* (Luke 23:43). His purpose remained to His last breath. *"Not My will, but Thine be done"* (Luke 22:42), "The Prayer that Changed the Universe."[77] Indeed, it did.

In 1806, five young men met at Williams College in Massachusetts to discuss a booklet written by William Carey entitled *An Enquiry Into the Obligations of Christians to Use Means for the Conversion of the Heathen*. While discussing Carey's challenge to take the Gospel to distant lands, a storm hit the campus—strong winds, rain, lightning, and thunder—forcing the group to run for cover and hide under a haystack. There, they prayed

---

[77] Frontlines, The prayer that changed the universe, *Christian Broadcasting Network*, March 2024, 4..

not for God to save them from the storm, but for something bigger than themselves. One student, Samuel J. Mills, suggested they all surrender to the Lord and follow William Carey's example by going to India as missionaries. Mills spoke seven powerful words that changed the course of their lives and the future of missions: "We can do it if we will." Prayer was necessary, but Mills believed that fulfilling God's purpose would require each man's commitment to go where God was leading and to do what God wanted done.

It is said, "There is a time to fish, and a time to cut bait." This was the time for *"fishers of men"* to bait the hook with the Gospel of Christ and cast their lines in an ocean of souls. That meeting gave birth to the American Board of Commissioners for Foreign Missions (ABCFM) in 1810. Fifty years later, twelve hundred missionaries were sent out under its banner to foreign fields. "By 1960, almost five thousand more had gone out to thirty-four different fields." The modern cross-cultural mission movement started under a "mound of hay" where five men, prompted and prepared by God's Spirit, humbly and obediently surrendered to the will, plan, and purpose of God for their lives.[78] It is the Spirit of God who gives us the drive to follow through on God's purpose and will—to move forward wherever God directs, to accomplish whatever God desires in, for, and through my life. The purpose of God is the key that unlocks the door to living a life that matters.

Jesus knew the reason for His mission and understood what was required. He would not fail. His eyes were fixed, His determination sure, His commitment resolute. He would not be deterred or denied from God's purpose. Neither should you be. In the face of false charges and under threat of crucifixion, Jesus declared, *"For this I have been born, and for this I have come into the world, to bear*

---

[78] Ross Paterson, A Prayer Meeting In A Haystack That Changed U.S. Church History, Copyright © 2023 *Field Partner International*, December 21, 2023.

witness to the truth" (John 18:37). Nothing Jesus did was meaningless. He was fully committed, all in, undaunted, and ready to live a life that mattered. He did, and so must you and I.

Singer/songwriter Carolyn Arends was on tour with Rich Mullins. She said, "I loved overhearing conversations at the autograph table; they often turned serious and urgent." She shared the following story:

> More than once, a fan asked Rich how to discern the will of God. Rich would listen and then offer an unexpected perspective. He'd say, "I don't think finding God's plan for you has to be complicated. God's will is that you love him with all your heart and soul and mind, and also that you love your neighbor as yourself. Get busy with that, and then, if God wants you to do something unusual, he'll take care of it. Say, for example, he wants you to go to Egypt." Rich would pause for a moment before flashing his trademark grin. "If that's the case, he'll provide 11 jealous brothers, and they'll sell you into slavery."

Carolyn added, "…loving God and others takes care of most of our discernment questions." God knows what He's doing. Get on board with His purpose and plans.[79]

The purpose of God will guide your every step, keep you on track, and help you zero in on what really matters. In the heart and mind of Christ, there were no doubts, no misgivings, no guessing,

---

[79] Carolyn Arends, You Probably Won't be sent to Egypt, *Christianity Today*, (July 16, 2013), retrieved from https://www.christianitytoday.com/ct/2013/june/consolation-prize.html

no wavering, and no second thoughts about what God was up to and the role Jesus was to play in God's story. He aligned Himself with God's desires and plans. He did it, lived it, set His boundaries, narrowed His focus, and made the sometimes hard choices to ensure the achievement and advancement of godly goals and objectives in His personal life and daily living.

"Soli Deo gloria"—for the glory of God alone—was the primary purpose of Christ in all things, including dealing with the devil in the desert. *"It takes more than bread to stay alive. It takes a steady stream of words from God's mouth"* (Matthew 4:4, MSG). Understanding. Obedience. Purpose. God's will and plan. Christ glorified God in the palaces of Rome, standing before Pontius Pilate (John 18:28-38), and in the healing of a crippled man by the pool at Bethesda (John 5:1-9). Every day, wherever He went, whatever He was doing or speaking, Christ's aim was to bring honor, glory, and majesty to the name of God, His Father. Elevate Him. Lift Him before the world. Point men and women toward Him as the only source of all that is good and right.

The centerpiece of all life and eternity is God in Christ. He alone is our single, most important purpose for getting up in the morning. Make God great in the eyes of the world. *"For everything, absolutely everything, above and below, visible and invisible... everything got started in him and finds its purpose in him."* (Colossians 1:16, MSG). We need to take a page out of Jesus' playbook, who made every breath He took count for more than lighting candles, singing hymns and cute little choruses, listening to boring, irrelevant sermons, and eating our fill at church dinners and dessert parties. Jesus prayed,

> **John 12:27-28, AMP** - *Now My soul is troubled and distressed, and what shall I say? Father, save Me from this hour [of trial and agony]? But it was for*

> *this very purpose that I have come to this hour [that I might undergo it. [Rather, I will say,] Father, glorify (honor and extol) Your [own] name! Then there came a voice out of heaven saying, 'I have already glorified it, and I will glorify it again.'*

A confirmation that the Son of God was on the right track. His entire life was so ordered and structured, aligned to do the right thing, to be useful and productive in carrying out and securing God's plan for His life and death—"It was *"for this purpose"* that He came *"to this hour."* May it be so in my own personal journey, from start to finish, glorifying God in all that I say and do. That's the plan. Find something to live for beyond yourself, and you will find something worth dying for. Let God fill in the details.

Gabe McGlothan, a young man of faith, a leader, and a member of the Grand Canyon University Men's Basketball team, put it like this on a Sports Spectrum Podcast: "My plan was, you know, to play D-I basketball, but I never thought it'd be this big of a blessing, and God poured into that. So, it's a beautiful thing..." He asked, "Who are you? What's your purpose? Is it to win a basketball game? Yes, that's important to me, but the more important thing is giving God the glory and shining His light..."

While discussing his 2020 baptism, McGlothan said, "You're talking about eternity here and giving up control of your own life. You think you have everything figured out, but in reality, God has the best plan for you. And you just walk in it in blind faith. Give Him control... I'll rock with my man Jesus until the end of time. And so, wherever He places my feet, I'll follow it."[80]

---

[80] Joshua Doering, Gabe McGlothan leads Grand Canyon through bold faith: 'I'll rock with my man Jesus Christ,' *Sports Spectrum*, February 28, 2024, retrieved from https://sportsspectrum.com/sport/basketball/2024/02/28/gabe-mcglothan-grand-canyon-bold-faith-jesus-christ/

We might consider a similar approach to life—following hard after the plan and purpose of God. Rock on, baby! Rock on! Live like it matters. Give up. Give in. Give out. Resign yourself to God alone and His will only, and make your life count in doing so. "Lord, I cannot do this unless Thou enablest me."[81] He will, and you can. God requires it.

---

[81] Brother Lawerence, *The Practice of the Presence of God*, Whitaker House; New Abridged ed. Kindle edition (June 1, 1982), 3.

"Where was God when my twins died??"
God's Answer: "Right here in the same place I was when My Son died......for you.

— **Bill Joselyn (friend),**
Facebook 2024

Chapter 6

LIVE IN THE PRESENCE OF GOD

John 8:29 - *"And he who sent me is with me. He has not left me alone..."*

John 16:32 - *"I am not alone, because the Father is with Me."*

Molly Lee was a passenger on a flight from Charlotte to New York. She noticed another passenger crying, scared of flying and anxious for her life. A flight attendant, Floyd Dean-Shannon, walked over to her, sat next to the woman, and took her hand. He quietly reassured and comforted her, saying, "Things are under control. No need to fear. You're going to be okay. You're safe." He added, "You know what? I got you. I'm gonna be there for you. Anything you need, you just let me know. But I guarantee the safety—if something wasn't right on this plane, we would never lift off the ground."[82]

So much like God and His presence in our lives. No need for an anxious spirit. God's promise is secure. "I got you. I'm gonna be there for you… always." A divine word of comfort straight from the throne room of heaven. God's attention has been, is, and will be forever fixed on you and me for time and eternity. *"I am with you all the days (perpetually, uniformly, and on every occasion), to the [very] close and consummation of the age"* (Matthew 28:20, AMPC). That's a long time—unending, eternal, forever and ever.

Jesus lived His life in the very presence of God, a significant factor in His success in completing His God-given mission for His life and death. And so it is for the rest of us. At no time was the *"Son of Man"* (Matthew 24:30) ever left to His own devices, even as He cried from the cross, *"My God, My God, why hast Thou forsaken (uncared for, neglected) Me?"* (Matthew 27:45-52). Dejected. Denied. Desperate. Yes, all of the above—distressed over the evil being done and with no deliverance in sight.[83] Heaven was silent. There was no move of God to rescue His Son. No release from the pain. No alternative plan was ever considered. He would remain *"a reproach of men… despised by the people,"* the object of ridicule, less than *"a worm"* (cf. Psalm 22:1-8), until He breathed His last and the plan of redemption was complete. God stayed the course. He had a plan, and He has a plan—a good one—for you to live a life that matters.

---

[82] *Haley Yamada, Flight attendant goes viral for helping a nervous passenger, WPVI-6ABC Action News*, Philadelphia, PA, February 22, 2023, retrieved from https://6abc.com/delta-airlines-flight-attendant-light-comforts-passenger-caught-on-video/12735115/.

[83] John Nolland, *The New International Greek New Testament: The Gospel of Matthew*, (Grand Rapid, Michigan: Wm. B. Eerdmans, 2005), XXI, F. Section 6. 3.

There was and is no other way. The sacrifice had to be made. The Lamb of God had to be slain. Redemption's plan had to continue until it was declared *"finished,"* and the temple veil was split in two (Matthew 27:51), allowing all manner of men and women to enter into the presence of a holy God.

The entire process was designed, orchestrated, and set in motion by God in eternity past. God's plan was, and is, true and right. No adjustments. No variations. No revisions. It was perfect and complete. Still is. God got it right the first time.

The Son of God, whose name was Jesus, would be born to rub shoulders with people, heal the sick and brokenhearted, preach the good news of God's love, mercy, and forgiveness, and to *"save His people from their sins"* (Matthew 1:21). Where once God walked the sacred halls of heaven with His Son, He would now walk the hills of ancient Bethlehem and beyond. Every step of the way, from the manger to the cross—where the Messiah would carry the full weight of damnation for all the sins of all humanity for all time (Isaiah 53:6)—the presence of God was there. *"I am not alone,"* Jesus declared, *"because the Father is with Me"* (John 16:32). The great *Elohim*, the great *I AM*, was present with His only Son. He was there at His side when He needed Him most to fulfill His divine mission and become redemption's sacrifice for all of mankind! He will be there for you. Period. You can't shake Him. And you may not want to try. For the divine presence comforts, encourages, and energizes you and me like nothing else can, enabling us to complete God's redemptive plan and purpose for our lives and to live a life that truly matters.

God the Father stood with Jesus in the Garden when the soldiers came to arrest Him. God would never run out on His Son. If He had, I might think that under certain dire circumstances, He might very well consider bailing on me, too. But He didn't run out on Jesus, and

He won't turn His face away from you and me now. He will stand with you. Christ was not alone in Pilate's courtroom. God was there, hearing His Son's accusers level trumped-up charges against Him. He was there when the crowd spewed vile hate and shouted for His execution. God was there at the foot of the cross as Roman soldiers pounded nails into His Son's hands and feet. He saw the spear thrust into His side. He saw the wounds. He heard Jesus cry, as He hung between heaven and earth, bruised and bleeding, *"Father, forgive them, for they do not know what they are doing"* (Luke 23:34, NIV). And when He breathed His last, God was there too, watching His Son, the Lamb of God, laid in a borrowed tomb, dead and gone... but not for long. He was there when the stone was rolled away from the mouth of the burial chamber that held His Son for three days. He was there when Christ conquered death and the grave, and rose as Victor and Redeemer. Such is the presence of God. *"I will never leave you,"* God promised. And He meant it. The presence and power of God serve His plan for your life and bring meaning and purpose to everything you do.

A. W. Tozer remarked, "I want the presence of God Himself, or I don't want anything at all to do with religion... I want all that God has or I don't want any."[84] Say no more. I get it.

Tradition tells us that Nero had planned to put Peter to death, but Peter was alerted to the threat by the other disciples. He fled for his life. On the way out of the city gate (probably Rome), Peter saw Christ walking toward him. Peter fell to his knees and asked, "Lord, where are you going?" Christ answered, *"I've come to be crucified*

---

[84] Jean Wise, A.W. Tozer: His Life and Quotes, Healthy Spirituality, March 28, 2017, retrieved from https://healthyspirituality.org/a-w-tozer/.

again."⁸⁵ The truest view of God often comes when we are at our lowest.⁸⁶

Peter was arrested and crucified upside down at his own request because he did not feel himself worthy to die as Christ did.⁸⁷ But Peter was not alone... ever. The presence of the resurrected Christ walked with him to the place of execution and brought him the inner strength, the will, and the ability to carry through to completion all that God required of him (John 21:17-18). The same holds true for you and me.

Even if the journey takes me to the horrors of a cross where I may suffer and die or to the heights of achievement and reward. God is never far from me. *"Rejoice in the Lord always. I will say it again: Rejoice...The Lord is near"* (Philippians 4:4). At no time, however, am I ever left to myself to tackle the mysteries and the sometimes harsh realities of life in a fallen world, riddled with malice, heartbreak, tears, and tragedy.

I am learning (though not fully there yet) to live in a conscious realization of the presence of God so I can live like it matters and better serve the interests of Christ's kingdom with my very life.

God may take me to the Lion's den, as He did with Daniel, to face hungry lions who want me for lunch, but I'm not going alone. Neither was Daniel. Neither are you. God was with him, and He is with you. The presence of God does not happen apart from His willing involvement and intervention. When Daniel was tossed into the den, God *"sent His angel and shut the mouths of Lions"* (Daniel

---

[85] John Foxe, *The New Foxe's Book of Martyrs*, (Gainesville, Florida: Bridge-Logos, 2001), 7.
[86] Glenn Beck interview with Max Lucado, End Times prophecies are being fulfilled, *The Glenn Beck Podcast,* November 2023, retrieved from https://www.youtube.com/watch?v=mg5JijoX10M
[87] Foxe, *op. cite.*

6:22). Daniel survived and went on to make his mark for God in a pagan land. The same God walks and talks with us.

Moses learned quickly that if he couldn't count on the presence of God in his life from the start of each day to its finish, he wouldn't take another step forward (Exodus 33:14-16). Good plan. God's presence was essential for victory and for Moses' success as a leader in guiding the people to the shores of the Jordan and into the promised land of Canaan.

Sometimes the presence of God takes me to the battlefield to pick a fight with a giant, but I don't go alone. God shows up at my side. I can *"prevail"* wherever God decides to place me (1 Samuel 17:50), whether it's before the Philistines dressed in battle array or standing without armor before a giant named Goliath, who defied and *"taunted the armies of the living God"* (1 Samuel 17:26, 36). Either way, God fights for me and with me to assure the outcome of the battle. The Hebrew word translated *"prevail"* means to become strong, mighty, and powerful, which is precisely what God's presence brings to my life and yours—the ability to succeed in any situation of God's choosing. There comes a newfound sense of confidence and an inner peace in knowing that *"Immanuel... God (is) with us"* (Matthew 1:23), and more specifically, with me each morning when I step out my front door to face the day. It is a profound truth that impacts daily life and our ability to serve His kingdom.

God's presence may direct me to the city gates of my enemies in Nineveh to boldly and effectively declare His message of forgiveness and mercy. I may try to run from His calling on my life, but I cannot outrun the *"presence of the Lord"* (Jonah 1:3-4) no matter how hard I may try. His presence will hunt me down wherever I am. Twice in verse three of Jonah chapter one, that phrase is repeated for emphasis. I may hide in the belly of a great fish, but

God will indeed find me, fish me out of its jaws, dry me off, and send me back on task to complete His mission—and He will be right there with me.

God may also put me on a ship bound for Italy that sustains heavy damage and sinks to the bottom of the Mediterranean Sea near the island of Malta (Acts 27:1-44). Panic is unnecessary, for God shows up with a message. His word is true. It is always the same: *"Don't be afraid. I'm here."* (Acts 27:23-24). Settle down. The crew of that doomed ship even had lunch together (Acts 27:20-44) in the hard rain and driving winds. The presence of God was, and is, real. There is a difference between feeling the presence of God and knowing that God is actually there in the fiercest of storms. What a wonderful and calming thought. One woman remarked, "I listen to Scripture for an hour when going to sleep, and I find that when I awaken during the night and first thing in the morning, God is still right there, front and center, and we start talking."[88] I think she's got something going for herself.

I came across this short verse. It is called *Trusting*, something we all need to embrace when dealing with God on a personal, visceral level. Written by Alice Marquardt, it speaks directly and powerfully to trusting God's person and presence to carry us through life, even in the darkest of hours, to the very place of His choosing. It reads:

> I do not understand it
> But I will keep trusting my Good Shepard
> Because I know He will not lead me
> Any place He does not want me to follow[89]

---

[88] Diana Chappell commenting to, *The Glenn Beck Podcast* End times prophecies are being fulfilled, November 2023.
[89] Alice Gray, *Stories for the Heart*, (Sisters, Oregon: Multnomah Books, 1996), 196.

Sherry Hubler graduated from Cedarville University in 1974, got married, and gave birth to her son, Joshua, who was born with Down Syndrome. At first, fear, disbelief, and sadness set in, but God gave peace in the middle of her turmoil and anxiousness. That experience prepared her for ministry with trauma patients. Her conclusions are revealing and encouraging.

> I know there are new challenges around every corner, but I also know God does not make mistakes. I have learned to turn it all over to Him—to listen to His voice as He gently speaks to my soul. I know that God is in control and that He gives us unexpected blessing in the midst of the challenges of life. I love Him and praise Him for what He has done in my life by giving me very special sons— my own and His.[90]

Her life mattered because God met her at the point of her need. Hardships are no barrier to God. His providence and presence made life count for Sherry, her children, and the many people whose lives were touched by her ministry.

Hagar, an Egyptian slave and handmaiden to Sarai, was distraught over recent events. She was fearful, alone in the wilderness, feeling cast off, used up, worthless, and *"despised"* (Genesis 16:5) by her mistress. Life had not turned out quite as she had hoped. *"An angel of the Lord found her"* (Genesis 16:7) in her distress. God was present. He saw her tears, listened to her story, and spoke comfort into her life. *"The Lord has given heed to your affliction"* (Genesis 16:11). She was not alone in the desert. Neither are we. Consequently, Hagar gave God a name: *"You are the God who sees me"* (Genesis 16:13). Yes, He does, and that matters. It's always mattered. My current life and my future are secure in the presence of God. He hears. He speaks. He acts. He is fully aware of

---

[90] Sherry Burns Humbler, Trusting, *Inspire,* Vol. 13, Issue 3, Summer 2003, 29.

where I've been, who I am, where I am going, and how I'm going to get there.

It was written of Moses that God *"used to speak to him face to face, just as a man speaks to his friend"* (Exodus 33:11). Perhaps the most important truth God ever told Moses was, *"My presence shall go with thee"* (Exodus 33:14), something every one of us can and must experience for ourselves—a life lived aware of God, the God who has personally entered into our daily affairs. No man can succeed disconnected from the presence of God. There are no exceptions. Moses became the greatest leader Israel has ever known. He took them on a wild journey of forty long, hard years to the banks of the Jordan and the Promised Land, with God at his side. Through all the failure, faithlessness, fear, and foolish behavior, God was there—present to see His people succeed as they followed His leading and guidance. When Joshua took over the helm of leadership, God promised him, *"As I was with Moses, so I will be with thee; I will not fail thee, nor forsake thee"* (Joshua 1:5). Good news. He never did. Just as God was with Adam and Eve in the Garden, with Enoch who walked with God for three hundred and sixty-five years, with Abraham on Mount Moriah, with Rahab within the city of Jericho, with Gideon, David on the battlefield, Stephen when he died, and so many others throughout human history, He will be present in my life and yours. The presence of God remains a key factor in living a life that counts.

Meshach, Shadrach, and Abednego were *"servants of the Most High God."* They had been condemned to die in a fiery furnace for refusing to bow before the image of the pagan king, Nebuchadnezzar (Daniel 3:16-28). But a *"fourth man" was* spotted in the flames. Nobody recognized Him or knew where He came from, but He was there, *"like a son of the gods"* (Daniel 3:25). Heaven had arrived, protecting and preserving God's men. The three walked out of the fire unscathed, unhurt, better than when they went in. No wonder. They lived in the presence of God, the God who walked with them through each day, every step of the way, even into the midst of the flames. Such is the presence of God at work in your life and mine.

God finds me wherever I am—in the valleys at my lowest points, in my failures and discouragements, or on the mountaintop in my successes, few though they may be. It makes no difference. He will not let me fend for myself. He will not write me off. I'd be in trouble (like you) if He ever did. He will not let me cry alone… ever. He will wrap His arms around me when I need it, and He will give me a swift kick in the pants when I need that, too. I cannot shake free of His love, though at times I have tried. His love, however, is unwavering and unending. He is accessible. He is approachable, and He always acts on my behalf, thoroughly involved in the events of my daily life.

For the Christian, there remains a consciousness of the divine presence, brought on by the power of God and the message of the Scriptures, where God comes alive for me, and I get to commune with Him on a level beyond casual. This is not simply another religious, mystical experience. *"Your Father knows,"* said Jesus, *"what you need before you ask Him"* (Matthew 6:8). It doesn't get much more personal than that. He is that close, close enough for me to reach out and touch the hem of His garment (Matthew 9:20-23), and experience the presence and power of God for myself.

Remember, He is never far from you or me… always and forever. Paul asked,

> **(Romans 8:35-39, MSG)** - *Do you think anyone (or anything) is going to be able to drive a wedge between us and Christ's love for us? There is no way! Not trouble, not hard times, not hatred, not hunger,*

> *not homelessness, not bullying threats, not backstabbing, not even the worst sins listed in Scripture...Jesus loves us. I'm absolutely convinced that nothing—nothing living or dead, angelic or demonic, today or tomorrow, high or low, thinkable or unthinkable—absolutely nothing can get between us and God's love because of the way that Jesus our Master has embraced us.*

The writer of the letter to the Hebrews concurs with Paul's conclusions.

> **Hebrews 13:5, AMP)** – *for He has said, 'I will never [under any circumstances] desert you [nor give you up nor leave you without support, nor will I in any degree leave you helpless], nor will I forsake or let you down or relax My hold on you [assuredly not]!'*

That's a game changer.

The phrase *"for He has said"* (perfect tense) suggests that the word spoken by God, the promises He made in the past, are still good and valid today and will remain good tomorrow and forever. Count on it. It's a fact. The presence and promises of God never come to an end. He is always here and there, and He will always be here and there... simultaneously. *You Never Walk Alone,*[91] —past, present, and future (cf. Deuteronomy 31:6-8). It doesn't matter where you are now or what you will face tomorrow; you will find God there, waiting for your arrival.

The verb translated *"leave,"* as in *"leave (forsake) you without support,"* in Hebrews 13:5 is preceded by three negatives in the

---

[91] Written by Oscar Hammerstein II for the musical Carousel, released in the USA in 1945. Later recorded by Gerry and the Pacemakers in 1963.

Greek text for emphasis, just in case we missed it: *"No. No. No."* God will never run out on you. He doesn't work that way. *The Amplified Bible, Classic Edition*, adds, *"I will not. I will not. I will not leave you."* A good word from on high. God will not ditch you. You cannot escape His touch nor His sight. God is not here today and gone tomorrow. You will never be rid of Him. His presence is my Security, my Refuge, my Stronghold, My Savior, my Guide and Counselor, *"a very present help in a time of trouble"* (Psalm 46:1). He is my Protector, my King, my Provider, the Shade on my right hand, the Keeper of my soul, and the Guardian of my every move *"from this time and forever"* (Psalm 121).

If God is not present in my life—if He doesn't stick around long enough and close enough to *"watch over"* me—then life is little more than a series of purposeless, cosmic accidents. Nothing matters. Best-selling author Max Lucado is right on target with his words.

> We (Christians) are always in the presence of God. There is never a non-sacred moment! His presence never diminishes. Our awareness of His presence may falter, but the reality of His presence never changes.[92]

Following the crucifixion of Christ and His subsequent resurrection, two disciples were heading to the village of Emmaus when *"Jesus approached them and began traveling with them"* (Luke 24:15). That's significant and applicable to us all. He walked with them, talked with them, interacted with them, and *"explained to them the things concerning Himself in all the Scriptures"* (v. 27). Better than a seminary education. But still, they didn't get it at

---

[92] Susan, Yet I will rejoice in the Lord | Habakkuk 3:18, *Fresh Grace for Today,* Feb 23, 2022, retrieved from https://freshgracefortoday.com/2022/02/23/yet-i-will-rejoice-in-the-lord-habakkuk-318/.

first—none of it. Christ called them *"foolish men and slow of heart"* (v. 25). I qualify on both counts—spiritually inept and slow. This was no gentle criticism; it was the truth. Like most of us, they failed to recognize the very presence of God as they journeyed forward. They missed Him, unaware that God was and is intimately involved in their daily lives.

Regardless of the day, the occasion, or the situation, God is always with me, whether I feel Him or not, whether I see purpose in my circumstances or I don't. His hand is always at work, bringing good. He promised He would, and that settles it in my mind and heart. He is personally directing my path, providing for my needs, protecting my life, and provoking me to holy action in every area of my life. *"The Lord is my Helper; I will not be seized with alarm [I will not fear or dread or be terrified]"* (Hebrews 13:6, AMPC). So wrote the author of Hebrews, whose recipients may have been under persecution and discouraged in their faith. Corrie ten Boom, a Dutch watchmaker who survived the horrors of a Nazi concentration camp, said, "I've experienced His presence in the deepest hell that man can create... I have tested the promises of the Bible, and believe me, you can count on them."

Living in the knowledge of the presence of God brings comfort to a troubled soul, courage and healing to a wounded heart, and confidence to an anxious spirit. I need not face the day taunted and terrorized by fears, stress, and worry, for the simple reason that God is present with me. He is in me, and He is for me. He is about me. That means liberty to make the most of my days, reaching forward to my potential to the praise of God's glory, even in the face of troubling, painful days I may never understand. His presence makes that a reality—the ability to overcome the things that would take me down and destroy or dismantle my life. There is nothing I can't talk with God about. His presence allows me to live in a "habitual, silent, and private conversation of the soul with God."⁹³ That is at the core of the *"abundant life"* Jesus promised to His disciples and followers (John 10:10). That's for me and you precisely because *"Christ lives in me"* (Galatians 2:20). I am not alone... ever. Neither are you.

Solomon points to a friend *"who sticks closer than a brother"* (Proverbs 18:24). No mystery who that is—God in Christ in me. Practice the presence of God.

Nicolas Herman (Brother Lawrence) was a soldier in the brutal Thirty Years' War (1618-1648). He barely survived a critical wound that left him horribly crippled and in pain for much of his life. Later, he entered a French monastery, where he learned to live daily, moment by moment, in the presence of God. He knew "by the light of faith that God was present, (and) he contented himself with directing all his actions to Him."⁹⁴

Lawrence "lived and walked with Our Father at his side" for over forty years. The presence of God found him and sustained him through every mundane event and trial he encountered. God had latched Himself to the man while he was in his mother's womb, right up to the day he died in 1691. He learned that the presence of God was, and is, the only way to live and make life count in the face of everyday challenges. Somebody once said, "Peace is not the absence of trouble, but the presence of God."⁹⁵

One woman recently wrote to tell me her story. In the summer of 2015, she lost her husband of forty-five years to a heart attack. It was sudden and unexpected. He was on life support for nine days

---

[93] Brother Lawrence, *The Collected Works of Brother Lawrence. The Practice of the Presence of God* (Kindle Edition), 5.
[94] Ibid, 14.
[95] *Preaching Today*, Peace in the presence of God, November 1998, retrieved from https://www.preachingtoday.com/illustrations/1998/november/5458.html.

when the decision was made to remove him from medical assistance. She wrote the following:

> My grief was overwhelming, and I couldn't find God in it anywhere…God gave us emotions and the necessity to grieve. It took me five years to reach full function, relying on God. It has now been nine years this coming June, and God is giving me an amazing life of ministry on many levels. To say that God was there from the start is correct, but the difficult five years helped make me who I am today by His grace. Looking back, I am thankful for that most difficult time. God has blessed me beyond what I could ever imagine.[96]

A testimony to the presence and power of God to repair and restore a broken heart. The presence of God made a difference and allowed a wounded soul to heal, get on with life, and live like it matters.

In J. R. R. Tolkien's epic, *The Lord of the Rings: The Two Towers*, King Théoden, who had taken refuge in the mountain stronghold at Helm's Deep, was eventually forced to **come to** terms with his own failure to lead and his inability to protect his people from impending danger, a humiliating defeat, and certain death.

An army bred by evil for war had breached the thick walls. A strong, vicious, merciless enemy, intent on methodically destroying the lives of men and women, rushed in for the final kill, swarming over the barriers. Helpless and hopeless, the king, dressed in battle array, looked out over the battlefield and saw his soldiers overrun, outnumbered, and dying. A slaughter was underway. On the verge

---

[96] Karen Roberts, responding to an excerpt (FB, March 12, 2024) from the book, , Lord Why? Questioning God When Life Hurts, by Sanford Zensen, (Wipf and Stock, 2024), 17-18. Used with permission.

of massive defeat, he lamented, "So much death. What can men do against such reckless hate?"[97]

Jesus gave us the answer: *"I am with you always, even to the end of the age"* (Matthew 28:20). The presence of God.

I arise today, through God's strength to pilot me,
God's might to uphold me,
God's wisdom to guide me,
God's eye to look before me,
God's ear to hear me,
God's word to speak for me,
God's hand to guard me,
God's shield to protect me,
God's host to save me from the snares of devils...
Christ with me,
Christ before me,
Christ behind me,
Christ in me,
Christ beneath me,
Christ above me,
Christ on my right,
Christ on my left,
Christ when I lie down,
Christ when I sit down,
Christ when I arise....[98]

Craft your day in the presence of God, and then go out with the rising of the sun, knowing that you are not alone, and live your life

---

[97] J.R.R. Tolkien, *The Lord of the Rings: The Two Towers* (the movie), New Line Cinema, released December 18, 2002., Screenplay by Fran Walsh, Philippa Boyens, Stephen Sinclair, and Jackson, based on 1954's *The Two Towers, the second volume of the novel The Lord of the Rings.*

[98] ST. PATRICK'S BREASTPLATE: PRAYER FOR PROTECTION, retrieved from chromeextension://efaidnbmnnnibpcajpcglclefindmkaj/https://parish.rcdow.org.uk/greenford/wp-content/uploads/sites/127/2020/03/St-Patricks-Breastplate.pdf

like it matters…because it does, and because you can. The presence of God… He is never MIA, missing in action. He is here *"from everlasting to everlasting"* (Psalm 90:2).

"God wants to be known by you, and you can know as much about Him as you have the appetite and desire to know."[99]

— **Louie Giglio**

---

[99] Louie Giglio, *Don't Give the Enemy A Seat At Your Table*, (Nashville, Tennessee: Passion Publishing, 2021), 171.

Chapter 7

MAKE A PERSONAL, INTIMATE RELATIONSHIP WITH GOD

THE HIGHEST OF PRIORITIES

John 8:19 (NLT) - *"Where is your father?" they asked. Jesus answered, "Since you don't know who I am, you don't know who my Father is. If you knew me, you would also know my Father."*

John 8:55 (NLT) – *"...you don't even know him (the Father)... But I do know him and obey him."*

One man, who considered himself a "reclusive dreamer," was asked, "How do you describe your relationship with God?" He responded, "My relationship could be described as—'ERROR 404 - God not found.'"[100] This is a computer error message which means

---

[100] Retrieved from https://www.quora.com/How-would-you-describe-your-relationship-with-God-and-why-is-it-important-to-you.

—the server cannot connect or retrieve a webpage or a document of some sort. It is frustrating, disruptive, and counterproductive, to say the least.

Jesus' experience and relationship with God, His Father, was much different. Their relationship worked—it was solid, close, deep, and intimate. It was the highest of priorities, as it must be for the rest of us. I want that for my own life.

God first reached out to a fallen Adam and Eve hiding in the bushes of the Garden of Eden, and He's been doing it ever since men and women first walked the earth. . All of humankind has been running away from God. We still are, but God had something better in store for His children from the beginning. He took the initiative (He always does) and went searching for a defiant, delinquent humanity. *"Adam, where are you?"* (Genesis 3:9). God's plan from the start was, and is, to connect with His children, even though they had made poor decisions and gone astray. The divine objective was to rescue, redeem, and restore man's broken relationship with his/her Creator, giving us a firsthand experience with the living God who loves us and wants the best for our lives. Fast forward thousands of years.

John recorded the most unimaginable, unexpected event: God, who otherwise was unrecognizable and unknowable to mankind, introduced Himself to the world. *"And God became flesh"* (John 1:14). He had to. We wouldn't know God if He hit us over the head with a brick. God explained Himself and showed us who He is and what He is like. Jesus showed up on our streets. *"God,"* said John in his gospel, *"let Himself out for us to see,"* in Christ (John 1:18). That was his assessment. In fact, Jesus said, *"If you knew me, you would also know my Father... Whoever has seen Me, has seen the Father" (John 8:19; 14:9).* That speaks volumes about their relationship One to the Other, as well as the identity and role of Jesus in presenting God to the world. Only God can explain (*exegete*) God. Let's settle that issue now.

Jesus knew His Father well. He said, *"I know Him,"* (John 8:55), as only God can know God—truly, deeply, intensely, infinitely! Three times in this verse, the words *"I have"* (or *"I have known"*) are repeated. These words convey a sense of being intimately acquainted, deeply familiar, and wholly connected to God the Father, experiencing Him on a level well beyond casual.[101] Jesus understood His Father fully and completely comprehended Who the Father was and is. He grasped the very essence of the Divine. He stood *"face-to-face"* with God, *"eye-to-eye,"* toe-to-toe, His very equal. Jesus had a real, down-to-earth, close, experiential tie to His Father. *"He was in the beginning with God"* (John 1:1-2). Jesus said of Himself, *"Believe Me that I am in the Father, and the Father is in Me"* (John 14:10, NLT). The miracles performed by Jesus bore witness to this divine connection. Both are God, as is the Holy Spirit (cf. John 14:26). Separate, distinct persons, yes, but One in essence and nature, in purpose, and fully functioning in agreement with each other—heading in the same direction, with the same mind, the same will, the same heart, and the same redemptive plan, each sharing the very core and substance of divinity.

A clear relationship exists within the tri-unity of God. God the Father *"sent His only Son into the world"* (1 John 4:9, ESV). The Son reveals the very character of the Father's love and mercy. *"For whatever the Father does, these things the Son also does in like manner"* (John 5:19). The Holy Spirit is also sent by the Father as *"the Helper"* to bring to *"remembrance"* all that Jesus has said (John 15:26). It is apparent that each Person within the Godhead is connected and intimately related, working together to serve the

---

[101] Willam F. Arndt and F. Wilbur Gingrich, *A Greek-English Lexicon of the New Testament and Other Early Christian Literature,* (Chicago, Illinois: The University of Chicago Press, 1957), 558-559.

advancement of the gospel and the kingdom of God. *"Hear O Israel, the Lord is our God, the Lord is one"* (Deuteronomy 6:4). The only One. Unique. Distinctive. Incomparable. We've never known, seen, heard, or met anyone quite like Him—far beyond human reasoning, understanding, and comprehension. Matchless. Absolute. Perfect in every way. And *"there is no other besides Him"* (Deuteronomy 4:35).That is what Jesus knew His Father to be. That's the way it should be when in a relationship of that magnitude and depth. They were, are, and forever shall be One.

Obviously, this is more than a superficial, shallow friendship or knowledge. There is a close, unbreakable, unmistakable relationship within the Godhead, with each member of the Trinity in sync and moving together in one accord toward one goal—mercy, forgiveness, love, and the redemption of humanity. Father, Son, and Spirit are all on the same page, in perfect relationship with one another. Jesus knew His Father's plan and understood His role within it. I desperately need that for my life too, especially if I'm going to live like it matters, above the average.

That is exactly the point—Jesus lived His earthly life within the context of a personal relationship with God the Father. It paid off, and it continues to pay off, with big dividends. We can do no less. We are, after all, *"sons and daughters"* of God in Christ (2 Corinthians 6:18). Therefore, it is imperative that we follow Jesus' example and do as Jesus did, get in alignment with our heavenly Father, walking hand in hand with Him—especially if we want more out of life beyond the artificial: the accumulation of trinkets and toys, diplomas and degrees, or the applause of the crowd. What truly matters is what God desires, and that begins with you and me, joined in community with Him—doing life together, courageously and confidently, no matter what comes our way or where it may lead, as long as it is with Him. Nothing else truly counts, fully satisfies, or, in fact, matters.

Saint Augustine (354–430 A.D.), Bishop of Hippo, recognized this centuries ago when he observed, "There is a God-shaped vacuum in every man (and woman) that only Christ can fill." It's a well-worn insight, but nonetheless the truth.

The Bible teaches that God searches me and knows me better than I know myself. It doesn't get any closer than that. He digs deep to reach my soul. He knows when *I sit down and when I rise up* (Psalm 139:2). He knows how I think, how I feel, how I live, what I do, and what I say. *"Before there is a word on my tongue… (God) knows it all"* (Psalm 139:4). David reminds us that *"God is familiar with all my ways"* (Psalm 139:3, NIV). In short, I can't "ghost" God. He knows me too well. That's been my experience, and I'm grateful for God's persistence and faithfulness in reaching down through the corridors of eternity and into my life. He simply will not let me go.

David wrote

> **Psalm 139:3-6, TPT -** *You (God) read my heart like an open book* (He is that close)…*You know every step I will take before my journey even begins. You've gone into my future to prepare the way, and in kindness you follow behind me to spare me from the harm of my past. You have laid your hand on me! This is just too wonderful, deep, and incomprehensible! Your understanding of me brings me wonder and strength.*

The psalmist writes of a level of intimacy with God beyond the ordinary, one that comes from a deep, loving, intimate association with Him—a close, personal encounter with the living God of all Creation, my Savior and Redeemer. I don't want just another religious, mountaintop experience that doesn't last: lighting candles, attending church and Sunday school because it is expected, or repeating rote, scripted prayers without much depth or personal meaning. I don't want to play church, tossing a few shekels into the offering plate as it passes by to ease my conscience, or having a form of religion but no real power, no real substance, no real experiential side of Christianity. I'm looking for a genuine relationship with God, the God Who rejoices when I rejoice and weeps when I weep (Romans 12:15), Who feels my broken heart, my disappointments and discouragements, Who *"keeps track of all my sorrows, collects my tears in a bottle, and records each one in a book"* (Isaiah 56:8, NLT), and teaches me everything I need to know to be successful in this life and the life to come.

That's a relationship with God, *"from whom all blessings flow,"*[102] an irrefutable connection between me and God, an undeniable partnership in life, a holy communion, a positive, practical interaction between Father and son (or daughter) that goes both ways. He is, after all, my Father, and He knows me.

He is nothing like my earthly father, who opted out of being a dad and deserted his two small children (and their mother) when they needed him the most—a selfish, self-centered, irresponsible man. But God is so very different and so much more. He actually wants me (imagine that) and draws me (and you) to Himself. He never bows out on His family. He never will.

On Saturday, July 13, 2024, the unthinkable happened in Butler, Pennsylvania, a quiet, rural community. A gunman opened fire on former president Donald Trump with intent to kill. He was hit. The shot grazed his right ear—a quarter of an inch may have ended his life. Pandemonium broke out, but by the grace, mercy, providence, and presence of God, he survived to see another day. God was on

---

[102] Thomas Ken, *Doxology* (17th Century), Public Domain, retrieved from https://www.britannica.com/topic/doxology.

the scene. Immediately, the Secret Service sprang into action. In the stands behind the president, a bullet struck Corey Comperatore, a former fire chief who attended the rally with his wife and two daughters. At the sound of the first shot, Corey dove over his family, wrapped his arms around them, and shielded them with his body, with no thought of his own safety. A bullet struck his head, and he died that morning. The governor of Pennsylvania said, "Corey was the very best of us."[103]

In the process, his heroic actions saved the lives of his family. He sacrificed himself. He died so they might live. The story sounds so familiar. At his funeral, a friend pointed out the obvious during his eulogy: "Corey loved his family… He did what a good father would do. He protected those he loved."[104]

So much like God, our heavenly Father, who loves you and me. *"Not willing that any should perish"* (2 Peter 3:9), He willingly stepped out from the palaces of eternity, threw Himself on a cross, and covered my sin with His life to save my soul. Incredible courage. Incredible love—God desiring an intimate relationship with the likes of me, one that extends into eternity. *"For God so loved (you and me) that He gave His only begotten Son… that we may have life everlasting"* (John 3:16). God *"dwelt among us"* (John 1:14) in the form of Christ, to *"give His life as a ransom for many"* (Matthew 20:28). He hung on a cross between heaven and earth, to redeem, rescue, protect, and shield those He loves from death and made it possible for us to live, to see another sunrise, to *"walk in newness of life,"* and ultimately, to see heaven open before

---

[103] Mirna Alsharif, Former fire chief killed at Trump rally hailed as a 'hero,' two more victims identified, *NBC News,* July 14, 2024, retrieved from https://www.nbcnews.com/news/trump-rally-shooting-victim-what-we-know-about-corey-comperatore-rcna161781.

[104] Michael Sisak, Hundreds attend vigil for Corey Comperatore, former fire chief killed at Trump rally in Pa., *Associated Press, WWHY PBS,* July 18, 2024, retrieved from https://whyy.org/articles/corey-comperatore-vigil-trump-rally-shooting/.

our very eyes that we might *always (through the eternity of the eternities)...be with the Lord!"* (1 Thessalonians 4:17, AMPC). A relationship that will outlast time and the boundless love, mercy, and grace of God and the heavens above.

> Ragan Sutterfield, an Episcopal priest, notes that the Scriptures all point to a God who seeks to be in relationship—a transformational connection with creation. It is through that relationship that we encounter Him... not as an idea but as an acting reality. Without God's Spirit, we would not find our lives renewed and transformed; without God's Son, we would not find a new possibility for human life joined to the divine life. Without this seeking, longing, relating God who sends, we would find only the god of the philosophers, winding clocks blindly in the sky. Instead, we find an Abba, a "God who so loves."[105]

An intimate knowledge of God, our heavenly Father, is the key to personal fulfillment and a successful, truly meaningful life.

In 1872, Annie Hawks, as a young housewife and mother of three, penned the following verse, which was later set to music: *I Need Thee Every Hour.* Words of comfort and dependence on God, which only come from knowing God and having been known by Him.

> I need Thee every hour,
> In joy or pain;

---

[105] Ragan Sutterfield, The Seeking, The Sending, *The Way We Practice*, May 22, 2024, retrieved from https://substack.com/@ragansutterfield?utm_source=substack&utm_medium=email.

Come quickly and abide,
Or life is vain.

I need Thee, O I need Thee;
Every hour I need Thee.
O bless me now, my Savior—
I come to Thee...[106]

Sixteen years later, Annie's husband died. Her words became her greatest comfort—words born in the arms of her Savior, trusting the One who loved her, and she, Him. She said,

> I did not understand at first why this hymn had touched the great throbbing heart of humanity. It was not until long after, when the shadow fell over my way, the shadow of great loss, that I understood something of the comforting power in the words which I had been permitted to give out to others in the hour of sweet serenity and peace.[107]

A relationship that stood the test of adversity and permitted her to move forward in her life.

Dr. Robert A. Cook, author, pastor, and former president of The King's College (NY), my alma mater, used to say at the close of every family radio broadcast and nearly every college chapel he attended, "Walk with the King and be a blessing." Nothing is more vital to the Christian life experience than a close walk with God in Christ. It produces strength for the day, courage to overcome my fears, hope in every trying circumstance I may have to face, and serves as a reminder of the rich blessings of eternity reserved in

---

[106] Annie Hawks (1835-1918), I Need Thee Every Hour, (*The Baptist Hymnal*: Nashville, Tennessee, 1991), 450.
[107] Robert J. Morgan, *Then Sings My Soul*, (Nashville, Tennessee: Thomas Nelson, 2003), 179.

heaven for those who live in relationship with God and approach life by serving the King and His kingdom. Religion is overrated and self-serving, but a relationship with God is what makes daily living count.

We must get to know this gracious God. A.W. Tozer asked,

> What is God like? What kind of a God is He?...God has provided answers; not all the answers, certainly, but enough to satisfy our intellects and ravish our hearts. These answers He has provided in nature, in the Scriptures, and in the person of His Son.[108]

God has made Himself known. He is accessible and available. The Throne Room is open for business. We have an audience with the King, who is glad to hear our petitions. My success and victory in daily living are contingent upon knowing God more fully and developing a relationship with Him. There is no other choice in the matter, and no other place to go. Everything hinges on my connection to Him. *"Come close to God,"* James wrote, *"and He will come close to you"* (James 4:8, AMPC). The closer I get to Him, and *"reach out and experience the breadth and length and height and depth (of God's love),"* the greater the opportunity to live *"full lives, full in the fullness of God"* (Ephesians 3:17-18, MSG).

Jailed for their faith, Paul and Silas were found *"praying and singing hymns to God"* (Acts 16:23-25). Of all places—a prison, locked away from all they once knew, stripped of their freedom and dignity. Incarcerated, but not without hope. They knew God, and more importantly, God knew them and where to find them. Their circumstances were of no consequence to God. He would not leave them to fend for themselves but would crawl into the dungeon with

---

[108] A.W. Tozer, *The Knowledge of the Holy*, (New York, New York: HarperCollins, 1961), 21-22.

them, get down in the filth of that awful place, and meet them there in the darkness of a prison cell, shaking the walls and foundations of the jail to get them out. He is faithful and true. They were His men on a divine mission, and God would see them on the road again to complete the tasks assigned by heaven. They had a relationship with God. He was with them. He was for them, and He was all they needed. Nothing more. No one else. They were tight with God.

We stand in awe of this God, who has come down into our world to be known by you and me. He didn't have to come or need to come. He chose to come of His own accord (Lord knows why?) to *"tabernacle"* (John 1:18) with us and link up with the likes of you and me. It was His good pleasure to do so, *"working in you (and me), giving you (and me) the desire and the power to do what pleases him"* (Philippians 2:13, NLT). God willingly gets His hands dirty handling my stuff. *"This is real love,"* wrote John, *"not that we loved God, but that he loved us and sent his Son as a sacrifice to take away our sins"* (1 John 4:10). That's a relationship I can live with.

God knows me fully, warts and all. That's a bit scary. He sees all the grit and grime of daily living, the "good, the bad, and the ugly" of our personal lives—yet, *O How He Loves You and Me.*[109] God has inscribed our very names on the palms of His hands (Isaiah 49:16). In short, *"He is not far from any one of us"* (Acts 17:27, NIV).

That is astounding—an incredible piece of life-changing information, to know that *"The Lord is near (at hand)"* (Philippians 4:5), that the Creator of the universe wants to be part of my life's journey. The God who desires to love me right where I am, then graciously takes my hand to lead me out of the mess I've made of

---

[109] Kurt Kaiser, *O How He Loves You and Me*, Word Music, LLC, 1975.

my life and guide me toward an exciting and fulfilling adventure, making each day count beyond anything I could have ever imagined. That's living like it matters.

Apart from a good, healthy relationship with God, nothing much of any consequence can happen. To know God on an informal level simply will not cut it. We must go deeper and get to know Him, hear Him, trust Him, love Him, and obey Him.

Dietrich Bonhoeffer wrote:

> One admires Christ… (but) one thing one doesn't do, one doesn't take him seriously. That is, one doesn't bring the center of his or her own life into contact with the claim of Christ to speak the revelation of God and to be that revelation. (Instead) One maintains a distance between himself or herself and the word of Christ, and allows no serious encounter to take place… (but) Christ claims my life entirely with full seriousness… Understanding this claim means taking seriously his absolute claim on our commitment.[110]

And therein lies the essence of developing a solid relationship with God and moving beyond religiosity—taking Christ seriously. When we do, we are positioned to bring meaning and purpose to our lives. Examples abound in the biblical and historical record. David wrote of his connection to God:

> **Psalm 34:17–19** - *The righteous cry, and the LORD hears, and delivers them out of all their troubles. The LORD is near to them that are of a broken heart; and*

---

[110] Eric Metaxas, *Bonhoeffer: Pastor, Martyr, Prophet, Spy – A Righteous Gentile vs. The Third Reich*, (Nashville, TN: Thomas Nelson, 2010), 83.

saves such as be of a contrite spirit. Many are the afflictions of the righteous: but the LORD delivers him out of them all.

David had a relationship with Almighty God as a boy tending his father's sheep. He learned of God at an early age while in the fields of Bethlehem. There, a young, ruddy-faced shepherd with little life experience discovered the faithfulness and power of God—a lesson that would carry him through the rest of his life. In fact, there was no choice in getting to know God better—not if he wanted to survive wild beasts, later a giant, or the rants and threats of a jealous king gone mad who wanted him dead. He needed God and a connection to Him to face each day with confidence (me, too), relying on God to help him do his job, rescue sheep, and prepare for a rough but profitable future. Eventually, he left the pastures and made his life count for so much more than the smell of sheep. He won a decisive battle with a few stones and a sling, killed a giant named Goliath, and routed the Philistine army. Victory was there for the taking. Later, David rose to the pinnacle of success and sat on the throne of the united kingdom of Judah and Israel. His relationship with God paid off. It always does.

I recently had the privilege of talking with my friend, Bob, a seventy-two-year-old man nearing his final days. Once a vibrant, strong, happy man, he was now slowly losing his battle with pancreatic cancer. He had spent the better part of his life serving God and ministering His love to people. Remarkably, he wanted to do more but couldn't. The vitality of youth was long gone. His strength was failing. Eating had become difficult. His gait was slow. At best, he was physically weak and unstable on his feet. I asked him, "What was the most important lesson you learned in the course of your lifetime?" He thought for a moment as his mind rustled through pages and decades of experience. Finally, he said, "The faithfulness of God. That's it. God is faithful and trustworthy. You can count on Him all the days of your life."

Some live their entire lives and miss that point. He did not. Years of walking with the King taught him well. His relationship with God was paramount.

Christian recording artist CeCe Winans sings of *The Goodness of God*—the God who is always faithful, who will always be there when the darkness of the night invades your soul, when you open your eyes and get your feet set on the floor to face the battles ahead, and when you fall exhausted at the end of a tough fight and a hard day. That's what my friend knew and experienced throughout his life—a firsthand relationship with God.

Soren Kierkegaard (1813-1855), the Danish theologian and philosopher, prayed:

> Father in Heaven! You have loved us first, help us never to forget that you are love so that this sure conviction might triumph in our hearts over the seduction of the world, over the inquietude of the soul, over the anxiety for the future, over the fright of the past, over the distress of the moment…You have loved us first O God, alas…without ceasing. You have loved us first many times and every day and our whole life through…When we wake in the morning— You are the first—You have loved us first, if I rise at dawn…You are there ahead of me, You have loved me first…and thus forever.[111]

---

[111] Richard J. Foster & James Bryan Smith, editors, *Devotional Classics*, (New York, New York: Renovare, Inc, 1990), 107.

Samson also had a relationship with God from his youth. *"The Spirit of the Lord came upon him mightily"* (Judges 14:6). But his life went awry and took a turn for the worse. He was no longer walking with God, and a clever pagan woman was able to deceive him. He lost everything—his physical strength, his moral compass, and his connection with God. However, he got what he wanted—God out of his life. *"He did not know that the Lord had departed from him"* (Judges 16:20). Perhaps the worst predicament any man could experience—isolated from God, the Source of his God-given strength. Samson had run out on the Lord of heaven and earth. No longer in touch with divine power, he had withdrawn from the very One who could bring victory to his life. God was out of the picture. It is what Samson willingly chose—life apart from God, a life left to his own vices and the consequences of his own behavior. He lived as he pleased, much like the old Frank Sinatra song, *I Did It My Way*. An approach to life that often ends badly.

Samson had grown callous, hard, unyielding, arrogant, and self-reliant—a formula for sure disaster. The results were predictable. Defeat was inevitable. His life was ruined, and he was a wreck.

The Philistines imprisoned Samson and took his eyes. Blinded and locked away in his own darkness, he spent his last days grinding wheat for his enemies, literally running in circles going nowhere fast—no direction, no purpose, and no power left in his bones to correct all that had gone wrong in his life. Samson was alone, cut off from the very God who could change his life and make things happen. At the lowest point of his life, he turned toward heaven once again to the God he once knew. He and God were back on talking terms, which was just what God had been waiting for.

One night, the Philistines brought Samson to their banquet hall to mock, shame, and gloat over his weakness and their victory. There was likely plenty of "trash talk" that evening. They tied him between the pillars that supported the Philistine temple of the god Dagon—a big mistake. Samson *"called to the Lord to remember him (and) strengthen him"* one last time. God heard his plea and answered. Samson literally "brought the house down," *killing more Philistines that day than he has killed in his entire life.* His relationship with God was restored, his strength renewed, and his spirit revived. There is no place God won't go to love and redeem the likes of Samson, you, and me—even in the midst of a pagan culture and temple. The love of God is unbreakable and unstoppable in the crucible of life. In that crucible, God can always be found.

Then there was Thomas, the doubter, who also followed Jesus and desperately wanted to recapture what he had lost—a personal, intimate connection to the Savior. After the death and resurrection of Christ, Thomas needed help to restore a faith shattered by life's trials. It is a familiar scene. I've been there. So have you.

Thomas watched Jesus die on a hill called *"the place of the Skull"* (Matthew 27:33). On that dark, gloomy day, before his very eyes, his hopes and dreams were dismantled. Crucifixion was cruel and final, reserved for the worst Roman criminals. Everything Thomas and the other disciples had wanted and prayed for over the last three years was lost, hanging on that cross. Nothing was left. Jesus was dead and gone, and the future for the disciples looked grim. Thomas, broken and distraught, cried, *"I won't believe it (the resurrection of Christ) unless I see the nail wounds in his hands"* (John 20:25, NLT). A week later, Jesus showed up, as He always does, and Thomas got what he needed. He experienced the presence and power of the resurrected Lord for himself. He needed a touch from God to move forward in his faith and to face the days ahead. We need no less.

A relationship with Christ is personal, as is the faith of every man or woman. The other disciples had already seen the risen Lord.

They were settled, their faith strengthened and anchored to the truth. The stone was rolled away, and the tomb was empty. But not Thomas. He needed his own faith and his own relationship with God. So do we. We cannot ride on the coattails of another when it comes to following Jesus. We do this for ourselves under the empowering and enlightening of the Holy Spirit. Jesus looked at Thomas and said, *"See My hands"* (John 20:27). Thomas looked intently and saw what he needed to see. He broke down, recognizing, "*My Lord and My God*" (John 20:28). His relationship with God was instantly restored and revived.

One morning, I awoke with the story of doubting Thomas on my mind. I pictured Thomas, emotionally and spiritually out of sorts, staring in wonder at the nail-pierced hands of the Savior. In my mind's eye, I saw the man break down in tears in that upper room, something I myself would have surely done at the sight of Jesus. Thomas looked a little closer at those wounded, merciful hands, and I thought (just conjecture here) that maybe—just maybe—Thomas might have remembered the words spoken by God and recorded by the prophet Isaiah long ago: "*See, I have written your name on the palms of my hands*" (Isaiah 49:16, NLT).

In that sacred, magnificent moment of truth, when faith comes to heal the soul riddled with fear and unbelief, could Thomas have seen his own name engraved on the wounded hands of Christ? Perhaps he also saw the names of Peter, James, John, Andrew, and the rest—and maybe even yours and mine, and every believer from the beginning of time to its close. It was a moment of divine revelation and spiritual clarity regarding God's care and concern for those He calls His own. In any case, a man was suddenly and supernaturally transformed from stale religion and dead orthodoxy into a vibrant, fully alive faith that brings real life—a life that matters, a life that will count for eternity and beyond.

Look a little closer; you, too, may find your own name inscribed on the palm of those nail-scarred hands. That's how I want to live—in a relationship with such a God, being and doing something significant and positive with the years I've been given. Jesus said, *"I know the Father."* Go thou and do likewise. It truly matters.

Christians under God will save or ruin the world, and that, in proportion as they live for the glory of God, or not, Christ represents them as "the light of the world," as "the salt of the earth." Thus plainly teaching, that if their "light be darkness," and their "salt have lost its savor," the world must sink down to hell in darkness... To glorify God, is the only object for which you have any right to live, for one hour. And you can live for no other purpose, with the least reasonable hope of being saved. (March 27, 1839. Prof. Finney's Lectures VII, Glorifying God).

— Charles Finney (1792-1875),
Presbyterian minister and leader of the Second Great Awakening in America (1805).

Chapter 8

GLORIFY GOD IN ATTITUDE AND ACTION

John 8:49, NIV – *"For I honor my Father…"*

John 17:2 – *"Glorify the Son, that the Son may glorify Thee."*

John 17:4 – *"I brought glory to you here on earth by completing the work you gave me to do."*

The Christian life is indeed to be lived glorifying God, a daily focus that has become little more than a shallow cliché in many circles, yet it remains, nonetheless, an extraordinarily important life principle. Jesus prayed, *"Father, glorify Thy name"* (John 12:28), and then set out to honor His Father by completing the holy tasks assigned to Him. In so doing, He drew the attention of a watching world toward the sovereign majesty of the God He served and loved. We can do no less.

Then, 21-year-old Sydney McLaughlin set a new world record during the 2020 Olympic Games. It was a gold medal performance. She became the only woman in history to run the women's 400-meter hurdles in under fifty-two seconds—a remarkable feat. She is a Christian and said:

"Records come and go; the glory of God is eternal. I no longer run for self-recognition, but to reflect His perfect will that is already set in stone. I don't deserve anything, but by grace, through faith, Jesus has given me everything."[112]

"Glory to God in the highest" (Luke 2:14), so the angels sang.

In the Sermon on the Mount, Jesus said how Christians were to live their daily lives: *"Let your light shine before* [in the sight of] *others, so that they may see your good works and give glory to your Father who is in heaven"* (Matthew 5:16, ESV). Whenever and wherever your life or mine is played out, the "glory" of God is at stake. There is no higher responsibility for the man or woman who goes by the name of Christian than to live right, in compliance with God's word and will, and reflect the person and character of God (love, joy, mercy, grace, etc.) in the world. *The Weight of Glory*[113] is heavy.

The Old Testament Hebrew word *kāḇôḏ* (kavod) is the term most commonly used and translated as *"glory."* It carries the sense of weightiness or heaviness. In other words, my actions and attitudes present the worth and value of God to the watching world. God is either admired and esteemed as fully praiseworthy, or He is cursed or ignored. The verb *glorify* means "to give weight to" or "to honor," that is, to recognize and acknowledge who God is, what He has

---

[112] Facebook post, August 4, 2024.
[113] C.S. Lewis, *The Weight of Glory, and Other Addresses*, (New York: The Macmillan Company, 1949).

done, what He is doing, and what He will continue to do in the future.

"God's glory," wrote Christopher Morgan, professor of theology and dean of the School of Christian Ministries at California Baptist University, "is the magnificence, worth, loveliness, and grandeur of his (God's) many perfections...(communicated) through his creation, image-bearers (that's you and me), providence, and redemptive acts."[114] The New Testament Greek word *doxa*, also translated as *glory,* adds the idea of reputation.

This is no ordinary god. This is the God Who transcends time and space, Who lives in the eternal past, present, and future, Who is from everlasting to everlasting. Time is of no consequence to God. He *"never changes or casts a shifting shadow"* (James 1:17). He remains the same, *"yesterday and today, and tomorrow"* (Hebrews 13:8*)*. You can count on it. You can count on Him. There is none like Him—majestic, magnificent, infinite, and wholly unique.

Jeremiah reminded an unfaithful nation of the reality of God, a message desperately needed for a people who had adopted the lifestyle and beliefs of a pagan culture: there is a God, and there is nobody or nothing quite like Him (see also Psalm 86:8-10).

> **Jeremiah 10:6-7, NLT** - *Lord, there is no one like you!*
> *For you are great, and your name is full of power.*
> *Who would not fear you, O King of nations?*
> *That title belongs to you alone!*

A contemporary message for the ages, then and now.

Paige Bueckers, a member of the University of Connecticut Women's Basketball Team, led her team back to the 2024 NCAA

---

[114] Christopher Morgan, The Glory of God, *The Gospel Coalition*, retrieved from https://www.thegospelcoalition.org/essay/the-glory-of-god/.

Final Four for an unprecedented twenty-third trip. They beat the University of South Carolina, the number one seed, to advance. It is an NCAA record. No other team had gotten that far so many times. Paige scored twenty-eight points and pulled down ten rebounds in that game. Afterward, she said in an interview before a national audience:

> "Just so much gratitude. I'm a living testimony. I give all glory to God. He works in mysterious ways."

Her testimony was clear. God was ultimately responsible for her success. She knew it. She said it. She lived it. She tore her left ACL last year and missed her entire season. But her faith held strong during the long months of rehab. She went on to say,

> Last year, I was praying to be back at this stage. He sent me trials and tribulations, but it was to build my character. It was to test my faith to see if I was only a believer in the good times. I just kept on believing. I did all I could so God could do all I can't."

And He did just that.

> "It's hard trying to make sense of it all now," she wrote on Instagram following her injury, "but I can't help but think that God is using me as a testimony as to how much you can overcome with Him by your side…I know I wouldn't be here without Him…I've just tried to shine and sort of make Him famous and use my light that He's given me to shine on Him.""[115]

---

[115] Kevin Mercer, Superstar Paige Bueckers leads UConn back to Final Four: 'I give all glory to God,' *Sports Spectrum*, April 2, 2024, retrieved from https://sportsspectrum.com/sport/basketball/2024/04/02/paige-bueckers-uconn-final-four-glory-god/?fbclid=

There is nothing so small that God does not take notice. There is nothing so big that God isn't bigger. He is more than any of us can conceive or imagine, and if we could see that far and wide, He would still be more. He is beyond compare. His knowledge is limitless. His thoughts are far above all creatures and creation. His goodness is without measure. His splendor is indescribable. His power is boundless. His love, grace, mercy, and forgiveness toward a wayward people (like you and me) are limitless and unending.

After God destroyed the armies of mighty Egypt, a watching nation of slaves asked the right questions on the beaches of the Red Sea,

> **Exodus 15:11** - *Who is like You among the gods, Lord?*
> *Who is like You, majestic in holiness, Awesome in praises, working wonders?*

The questions are rhetorical. The answer is no one. Nothing. He is absolute, and there are no others worthy of worship and honor. There is none but Him. *"For I alone am God! I am God, and there is none like me"* (Isaiah 46:9, NLT).

Australian Dr. Sean George, on a routine visit to an outlying medical clinic, went into cardiac arrest and suffered a heart attack. He was treated by two doctors and several nurses, who attempted to restore the function of his heart and save his life. His heart effectively stopped for an hour and a half. He was dead and gone. After thousands of chest compressions and thirteen shocks from a

---

IwAR1i9crLp6fBjX_b_3tSZVio40dT8NQOD9AV5mnzdBLQWqpQjSRsK3v9yts_aem_AWlSRvKlh-LTAUK4-
m4QM9OLRQpMSpgC1LXYp1YORikFPGUMqCTpg0InJYPUmJ3Fz0a-ZLbQ2Aoamlzj-S-emZnm.

defibrillator, his heart's ECG was flatlining, and eventually, treatment was suspended.

Sherry, Sean's wife, was called to the hospital, informed of the dire situation, and advised to say her goodbyes. Instead, she walked into the resuscitation room where her husband's lifeless body lay. She came to the side of his bed, reached down, gently grasped her husband's cold hand, and prayed—just a simple prayer, packed with divine power and raw courage: "Lord, Sean is only thirty-nine years old. I am thirty-eight years old. We have a ten-year-old boy. I need a miracle." And a miracle was what she got. He immediately began to breathe. Signs of life appeared. His heart rate returned, and hope became reality. The medical prognosis, however, was not encouraging. Twenty minutes without blood supply and the "brain would suffer irreparable damage. " Against all odds, Sean fully recovered. God had acted. The medical records verify the events of the day. Sean had no doubt of God's involvement in his recovery. He said,

> There aren't many well-documented cases of patients being clinically dead for so long, returning to life with their memory perfectly intact and without any neurological problems at all. Medically this is impossible; it could only be done by God.... I believe I am only alive because God has done an amazing miracle.[116]

"To God Be the Glory, Great Things He Has Done...Praise the Lord. Praise the Lord. Let the people rejoice."[117] Chalk up one more for heaven and the sovereignty, mercy, and glory of almighty God. There is no other reasonable explanation. There is none like our

---

[116] Eric Hatfield, Dying doctor recovers after prayer (Dr Sean George), *Is There A God*, February 11, 2022, retrieved from https://www.is-there-a-god.info/life/seangeorge/.
[117] Fann Crosby (1875), *To God Be the Glory*, Public Domain.

God. *"The Lord has done great things for us, and we are filled with joy"* (Psalm 126:3, NIV).

Making God famous in the world is the task assigned to every believer. We are clearly called to declare, without compromise or hesitation, our recognition of God and the role He plays in our daily lives. Glory and greatness, splendor and power are all intertwined, producing awe, wonder, and reverence in all who witness God at work. John Piper said in an interview:

> "I believe the glory of God is the going public of his infinite worth. I define the holiness of God as the infinite value of God, the infinite intrinsic worth of God. And when that goes public in creation, the heavens are telling the glory of God, and human beings are manifesting His glory because we're created in His image, and we're trusting His promises so that we make Him look gloriously trustworthy.[118]

He is that and more. We must not shy away from pressing His name forward. We are in the business of making God look good. However, it must be said that God does not act out of a self-centered motive to elevate Himself or grab all the headlines. No, His actions flow from His abundant, unending, sacrificial love and grace, His relentless mercy, His persistent faithfulness, and His divine will to redeem and *"set at liberty"* His people from all manner of destructive behaviors and moral decline. He is immeasurably good, infinitely wise, and zealous for our well-being and success. Somebody needs to know that.

How others see God is directly tied to the life you and I are living. The world will assess your values, your belief system, your

---

[118] John Piper, What is God's glory? *Desiring God, July 6. 2009, retrieved* from https://www.desiringgod.org/interviews/what-is-gods-glory.

goals, and your approach to daily living—how you are under pressure as a person, a friend, a neighbor, and a professional. Your loyalties, your hopes and dreams, the consistency and quality of your faith, the depth of your compassion, and your love for people are on the line. The name of God hangs in the balance. Whether you like it or not, your entire life is a revelation of God to the world. Jesus said, *"You will know them by their fruits* (Matthew 7:15-20). Indeed, the glory of God is demonstrated every day in the little things, by the fruit you and I bear (love, joy, peace, patience, faithfulness, etc.). How much I am like Jesus in my personal, day-to-day living tells the true story. I have a way to go in that regard.

As the ancient world observed how Christians lived and died, they labeled them *"Christ-followers"* (Acts 11:26), and that they were without question—men and women who became an extension of Jesus in the world, on the streets where they lived. They were known as *"disciples"* (Matthew 28:19), *"fishers of men"* (Luke 5:10), *"brethren"* (Galatians 1:2), *"saints"* (Philippians 1:1), the *"beloved of God"* (Romans 1:7), and *"ambassadors for Christ"* (2 Corinthians 5:20), just to name a few.

The world watches every move Christians make. They hear what we say. They observe our attitudes and actions and will quickly hold us accountable. You can bet on that happening. We carry God's banner into every circumstance—trial, failure, and success. Everywhere the first-century church went, they took God's reputation with them—into jails, to the streets, into the temples of the religious elite, and even into the Roman arena, where they were mocked, scourged, *"stoned, and sawn in two."* It was said that *"the world was not worthy"* (Hebrews 11:32-38) of such people. Not much has changed except for the arenas where the world observes followers of Christ living out their lives. Our reputation matters. How we represent God in life and death matters.

My life's message must come through loud and clear: God is worthy of praise, honor, respect,[119] my finest effort, my very life—and yours. The Apostle Paul wrote, *"...whatever you do, do all to the glory of God"* (1 Corinthians 10:31). God's glory remains the focal point of all life. Glory belongs to God and God alone. *"I am the Lord; that is My name! And My glory I will not give to another, nor My praise to graven images"* (Isaiah 42:8, AMPC). Give credit where credit is obviously due. It's never been about you and me anyway. Humility looks good on us all.

Jesus said to His Father, *"I glorified Thee on the earth* (Here is how), *having accomplished the work which Thou hast given Me to do"* (John 17:4). Answer the call of God upon your life. Serve Him in the place of His choosing. Fulfill the divine mission committed to you and no one else, and do what He sent you to do, lifting the name of Jesus high for the world to see as you move through each day. Bring to light the best of God for others to see and experience—His grace, mercy, compassion, love, faithfulness, care, and His power, plans, and promises. All of it and more. *"Christ in you (in every believer, in me, and* in *you), the hope of glory"* (Colossians 1:27), is how God chooses to *"make known"* the *"mystery"* of His Person. Peter's first letter instructs followers of Christ to *"Live such good lives among the pagans that, though they accuse you of doing wrong, they may see your good deeds and glorify God on the day he visits us"* (1 Peter 2:12, NIV). Consequently, I play a significant role in presenting the grandeur and reality of God to the world. It matters how I choose to live.

Pat Robertson, founder of the Christian Broadcasting Network, whose ministry spans the globe, drives the point home: "When you give, smiles grow bigger. When you care, homes are happier. When

---

[119] Allen C. Meyers, Eitor, *Eerdmans Dictionary of the Bible* (Grand Rapids, Michigan: W.B. Eerdmans, 1987), 420.

you comfort, the hurt goes away. When we all come together to love, miracles happen."[120] In other words, when you live like Jesus and bring the love of God to the brokenhearted, the lonely, the sick, the blind, the lame, and to those who *"hunger and thirst for righteousness (uprightness and right standing with God)"* (Matthew 5:6, Phillips), and offer the Good News of God's mercy and forgiveness to those morally bankrupt and in need of a new start and a new life (and that's all of us), the glory of God is extended to the far reaches of the world, particularly to my little corner of the cosmos. We bear witness to the goodness of God (2 Corinthians 9:12-13) and attest to His very existence and character. A weighty matter, for sure.

Unfortunately, we have erred. Our theology is anything but biblical. We've often portrayed and presented God solely as an all-too-familiar friend, a buddy to hang with, or a celestial Grandfather with white hair, kind eyes, and a gentle voice—and not much more. Sometimes, in our self-righteousness, we present God as harsh, unkind, and vindictive, leaning over the balconies of heaven, throwing lightning bolts at people who don't measure up to our standards of behavior. We seem to enjoy roasting people over the fires of hell. But none of that works very well. Jesus set the record straight.

> **Luke 18:11-13, MSG** - He told his next story to some who were complacently pleased with themselves over their moral performance and looked down their noses at the common people: "Two men went up to the Temple to pray, one a Pharisee, the other a tax man. The Pharisee posed and prayed like this: 'Oh, God, I thank you that I am not like other

---

[120] CBN Overview 2022 video, A Global Non-profit Ministry, *Christian Broadcasting Network*, 2022, retrieved from https://www2.cbn.com/ministries.

people—robbers, crooks, adulterers, or, heaven forbid, like this tax man. I fast twice a week and tithe on all my income.'

Meanwhile, the tax man, slumped in the shadows, his face in his hands, not daring to look up, said, "God, give mercy. Forgive me, a sinner." In essence, we have lost sight of God's greatness, His grace, and His glory. We no longer fall prostrate before His majesty. When Isaiah saw *"the King, the Lord of hosts*," and the presence of *"His glory,"* high and lifted up (exalted), seated upon the throne of the universe, the prophet shrank down, bowed low, a man in utter despair. He was dejected, stripped of his dignity and self-respect. He was doomed, undone, as good as dead, and he knew it. No man could raise his head in the presence of the holiness of such a God, whose "glory" fills *"the whole earth"* (Isaiah 6:3). Isaiah cried out in utter dejection, an "annihilating anguish of self-condemnation."[121] No arrogant pounding of his chest. All Isaiah could muster was, *"Woe (oy) is me, for I am ruined (lost, destroyed, silenced)"* (Isaiah 6:5). *"Woe,"* not "Wow," is a word of rejection, not of God, but of Isaiah himself. His self-assessment was brutal. He was a man of *"unclean lips,"* an unworthy soul, a guilt-ridden conscience, a man with dirty hands… without merit—less than what he should be or could be, a man who caught a hint of what he must be before God but wasn't. In truth, he was speaking for the rest of us. One does not truly see himself until he first sees the majesty of the holy God. His glory changes everything.

Doctor Luke records (Luke 5:17-26) the healing of a crippled man. He was paralyzed and could not walk. Life was hard. His only chance was Jesus. He needed a miracle, and the crowd was looking on. Some friends lowered the man down through the roof and *"set*

---

[121]C.F Keil and F. Delitzsch, *Commentary on the Old Testament in Ten Volumes,* Vol. VII, (Grand Rapids, Michigan: William B. Eerdmans, 1978), 196.

him down in front of Him (Jesus)" (Luke 5:18-19). Seeing their faith, Jesus acted. *"Your sins are forgiven... rise, take up your stretcher, and go home"* (Luke 5:20, 24). The response of the man and the crowd is noteworthy. The man, who once could not walk, got up *and "went home, glorifying God"* (Luke 5:25). The people were astonished and astounded. They could not fully comprehend what they had just seen with their own eyes. The only plausible explanation? God. Nothing else made sense. God had stepped in, and the lame man proclaimed the reality of the work of God in his life, and did so with great joy and wonderment. Who wouldn't?

Either I approach life from a biblical perspective and consistently live a life of faith in Jesus Christ for the glory of God or I buy into a world system antagonistic to the truth of the gospel and go my own way, ignoring the sovereignty of God. Whichever way I choose, the world is watching. They will view the reality of God and the genuineness of my Christian life and faith based on how I live. We bear witness to the person and power of God by our lives, or we ruin and destroy His reputation. We honor Him by living under the authority of His word and show Him to be Lord, or we dishonor Him with poor decisions and behavior that fall well beneath kingdom standards. A.W. Tozer said, "God is looking for men in whose hands His glory is safe."[122] I couldn't have said it better. Tozer was right. You and I hold the glory of God in the palm of our hands. That's heavy stuff.

Back to the 2024 NBA championships and the Boston Celtics' head coach. Joe Mazzulla arrived at the post-game interviews. The room was packed with reporters from across the world. The coach walked in wearing a T-shirt that read, "But First... Let Me Thank

---

[122] Charles Heck, My top 10 A.W. Tozer-isms, *Worldly Saints*, December 11, 2018, retrieved from https://worldlysaints.wordpress.com/2018/12/11/my-top-10-a-w-tozer-isms/.

God."[123] The message was clear—glory and honor ultimately belong to God and no one else. His name was and is to be praised, exalted, and magnified above all, and it was. At courtside, before the TV cameras and millions of fans, a simple T-shirt slogan said all that needed to be said, and a championship trophy was lifted high over the head of the coach, marking the achievement and giving credit where credit was due—to the God who made it all possible.

Three words define the story of redemption (Luke 2:14), which is the gospel story of the blessing and grace of God extended to all in Jesus Christ. Three words also sum up the unexpected, miraculous story of my life, and I suspect yours too—every success, every athletic trophy I took home, every academic degree hanging on my office wall, every accolade, achievement, or award I've ever received, every step I climbed, every milestone I reached, and every experience (the lows and the highs) I've gone through over the years that pushed me and pressed me to grow and mature—all of it can be summed up in just three words: "He did it!" I need a T-shirt like that. David examined his own life, wrote a song, and sang it to himself, *"Bless (speak well of) the Lord, O my soul; And all that is in me, bless His holy name"* (Psalm 103:1), and so I shall. I am forever indebted to the God who *"satisfies your (my) years with good things"* (Psalm 103:5). He has done just that. Let my soul sing, *How Great Thou Art...*[124] Let my light shine on the splendor of God.

John got a peek into heaven and recorded his vision in the Revelation of Jesus Christ. What he saw and heard defies description, but he tried. He wrote:

---

[123] Sports Spectrum post, *Facebook,* June 18, 2024, retrieved from https://twitter.com/zakisolja/status/1803030034447237503.
[124] Stuart K. Hine, How Great Thou Art, , *The Baptist Hymnal,* (Nashville, Tennessee: Convention Press, 1991), 10.

Revelation 5:11-14, ESV - *Then I looked, and I heard around the throne... the voice of many angels, numbering myriads of myriads and thousands of thousands, saying with a loud voice,*

"Worthy is the Lamb who was slain,
to receive power and wealth and wisdom and might
and honor and glory and blessing!"

The rest of the universe then piped in on the chorus.

To him who sits on the throne and to the Lamb
be blessing and honor and glory and might forever
and ever!

The final word came and echoed across the heavens like rolling thunder. Eternity shouted, *"Amen!"*—"So be it!"

Dr. Ming Wang (MD from Harvard and a PhD from MIT in laser physics), founder of the Wang Vision Institute, is the subject of the movie *Sight* (Angel Productions, May 2024). It tells the story of a young Chinese immigrant who overcame the greatest of odds, surviving the Chinese Cultural Revolution (1966-1976). During that time, the government of Mao Zedong severely restricted educational opportunities. Schools and universities were shut down, books were burned, and twenty million young people were being shipped off to labor camps. Ming faced poverty and an uncertain, bleak future, yet later became a world-renowned eye surgeon. God had given him a brilliant mind and the opportunity to study at Harvard Medical School and MIT, where he graduated with the highest academic honors. His is a story of a miracle-working God.

Ming arrived in the United States with fifty dollars in his pocket, no sure plan, no clear direction or guidance, and without knowledge of or belief in God. At the time, he was an atheist. All he knew and believed was that science held the answers to the deepest needs of humankind—certainly not God or religion. However, God had His hand upon the young man.

Divine providence placed a number of people into Wang's life who challenged his disbelief in the existence of God. He weighed the evidence. His eyes were opened, and he converted to Christianity. He said he had learned two important lessons that changed his life and inspired his research.

Lesson one – *God has a plan and purpose for us all—the faith and confidence to know that God is watching over each of us* (you, me, and Dr. Wang). He said, "I think the real challenge of being a Christian isn't asking God and getting what you want, but asking God and accepting what He gives." The authority of God governing the lives of men and women is paramount to daily, successful Christian living.

Lesson two – *God created a world perfect without contradiction, with each part designed intentionally and with a specific purpose*—an important concept in medical research. The lesson is clear.

Psalm 19:1-2:

The heavens proclaim the glory of God.
The skies display his craftsmanship.
Day after day they continue to speak;
night after night they make him known.

The splendor and glory of creation more than adequately reflect the Creator Himself,[125] whose wisdom, providence, and trustworthiness empowered Dr. Wang's extraordinary career. God took a nobody with nothing and made him somebody with the capacity, knowledge, skills, and compassion to help some fifty-five thousand patients from over forty states and fifty-five countries—an ordinary man raised up from the streets, living an extraordinary life, bringing sight to the blind and visually impaired.[126] Only the grace, power, and intervention of God could accomplish such things in the life of an individual who truly honors His heavenly Father by the life he or she chooses to live.

Make a good choice. You and I hold the glory of God in our hands. Live a life that matters, glorify God every day in a world that so desperately needs to see Him. Let your "light" shine brightly, and so honor Him before the world.

---

[125] Written by Wang Foundation for sight restoration, Dr. Wang's testimony as a scientist and as a Christian, *Wang Foundation*, retrieved from https://wangfoundation.org/christian-outreach-to-china/7-articles/static-pages/7-dr-wangs-testimony-as-a-scientist-and-as-a-christian.html.
[126] Ibid.

"The largest results of praying come to him who gives himself, all that belongs to himself – to God."[127]

– E.M. Bounds,
One Minute Devotions: The Power of Prayer

---

[127] E.M. Bounds, Wholeness through prayer, *One Minute Devotions: The Power of Prayer*, (China: Christian Art Publishers, 2007), January 1.

Chapter 9

TALK WITH GOD...A LOT

John 17:1, 10, NIV – *"After Jesus said this, he looked toward heaven and prayed... All I have is yours, and all you have is mine."*

I need help. Prayer has always been a struggle. My mind wanders, my thoughts are jumbled, my focus is lacking, and my faith is unsteady. I'm too easily distracted and discouraged if I don't see immediate results or if God turns down my requests. I give up all too quickly. I understand the disciples when they begged Jesus, *"Lord, teach us to pray"* (Luke 11:1, NLT). I could use some lessons. Billy Sunday once prayed, "Lord, save us from off-handed, flabby-cheeked, brittle-bone, weak-kneed, thin-skinned, pliable, plastic, spineless, effeminate, ossified, three-karat Christianity."[128] That man wasn't afraid to speak his mind to God.

---

[128] Margaret Bendroth, Why women loved Billy Sunday, Religion and American Culture: A Journal of Interpretation Vol. 14, No., (Cambridge University Press, Summer 2004), 251-271.

It was just before game time. The Bryan College men's soccer team was in the locker room, getting ready to face its cross-town rivals in an intercollegiate match, a winner-take-all playoff match. I asked one of my seniors to pray and lead us out onto the field. He was a tough, rugged kid, tenacious, a hard-nosed player, highly skilled, and captain of the team. I was glad he played for me. The team stood together in the locker room, bowed their heads with arms draped over each other's shoulders as he prayed. I will never forget it. "Lord, if today we must die, let us do so as warriors! Amen." That was it—nothing else. I smiled. I loved it. His prayer was raw, brutally honest with God, ferocious, and bold beyond measure. He was ready to go to war. He knew the cost of victory, but he also knew what he wanted from God and went after it. It was a good lesson for me. God was teaching me to pray with boldness, passion, and forthrightness. That kid had it, did it, and I needed it. No namby-pamby prayers. No weak-faith "maybes." Just straight, fearless, hard talk with God, leaving the results to Him. It's a viable principle for living a life that matters. By the way, we won the game in overtime. No credit to my coaching. Those kids played with abandonment.

Catholic writer and mystic Thomas Merton (1915-1968) once asked, "What is the use of praying if, at the very moment of prayer, we have so little confidence in God that we are busy planning our own kind of answer to our prayer?"[129] That's me—a man who often prays with a backup plan in mind, just in case things don't go the way I want, which, by the way, is quite often. Unfortunately, I have come to expect rough going in my conversations with God. But I have also discovered that God is the God of surprises. Though my attempts at reaching Him and connecting to heaven are considerably feeble and, at times, ineffective, He always manages to catch me off guard and do the unexpected. I am forever shocked by God's grace to fill in the gaps of my prayers and grant me the best of His

---

[129]Thomas Merton, *Thoughts in Solitude*, (New York: Farrar, Straus, & Cudahy, 1958), 35.

decisions, which sometimes are not what I originally asked for or wanted. After all, I have my plans. God has His, and they're better—always. He does, however, give me all that I need out of the storehouse of His riches to face the day and fill the holes in my heart.

When life doesn't seem to cooperate, or I'm backed into a corner with no apparent escape, I have mistakenly approached God as my "last resort." God is a lot of things, but a "last-ditch effort" is not one of them. I should know better. God must be my first move, not my last. He has an inexhaustible supply of resources at His disposal. The problem isn't God's—it's mine. Questionable motives, suspicious intent, lackluster faith, and an impure heart. Fundamentally, I have not because I ask not (James 4:3). No tenacity, no fervency, and a focus solely on selfish desires and self-serving petitions. William Booth (1829-1912), the founder of the Salvation Army, said,

> *You must pray with your might... That does not mean saying your prayers, or sitting gazing about in church or chapel, with eyes wide open, while someone else says them for you. It means fervent, effectual, untiring wrestling with God. It means that grappling with Omnipotence, that clinging to Him, following Him about, so to speak, day and night, as the widow did to the unjust judge, with agonizing pleadings and arguments and entreaties, until the answer comes, and the end is gained.*[130]

I would be a fool to do otherwise.

---

[130] Dale A. Robbins, What is effectual fervent prayer? Victorious Publications, July 29, 2024, retrieved from https://www.victorious.org/pub/prayer-fervent-effective-187#google_vignette.

Prayer is seeking the face of God in the midst of the mundane affairs of daily life or against impossible odds—situations in which God specializes. Prayer is intimacy with Him, talking over both the big and small things that weigh heavy on my heart, and bearing my soul to the One who never gets tired of hearing me. Sometimes, if I'm honest, my prayers resemble a spiritual tantrum—pulling on God's beard, pounding on His chest, yelling, screaming, crying, kicking, and stomping my feet like a spoiled brat just to get His attention and maybe force His hand. It's not a pretty sight. But none of that works very well anyway. God is not hard of hearing, nor does He respond to human pressure or emotional manipulation. He does what needs to be done—no more, no less, every time, all the time, and on time.

If I don't get what I want, which may or may not happen, let it be clear that God takes no pleasure in my demise or fall. He is interested in my success as His image-bearer, as a human being, as a follower of Christ, and as His representative in the world.

At the Red Sea, Moses prayed while the people complained to God, fearing for their lives. The Egyptians were closing in for the kill. It must have been terrifying. The Israelites were shaking in their Jewish sandals like a bunch of sissies at the sight of Egypt's war chariots. Where did their faith go? I'm not sure I would have reacted differently. But Moses spoke candidly, without mincing words. He got straight to the point: *"Shut up, boys! Stop your whining. Stand up like men* (my paraphrase), *and see the salvation of the Lord, which He will accomplish for you today…The Lord will fight for you* (Imagine that) *while you keep silent"* (Exodus 14:13). I love the *"keep silent"* part. It means, "Shut my mouth. Quit my complaining. God's got this." That's an effective approach for daily living. Whether I'm facing immediate stress or anxiety about tomorrow, I need to encounter the reality of God to calm my spirit and settle my thinking.

First-century Christians were no exception to human weakness. Under threat of persecution, the Apostle Paul instructed the church at Thessalonica, *"Rejoice always."* Why? Because you are about to enlist the King whose power, authority, and wisdom are unmatched and unlimited. *"Pray without ceasing."* Keep asking. Don't quit so easily. *"Give thanks in all circumstances."* Trust Him in every situation, *"for this is the will of God in Christ Jesus for you"* (1 Thessalonians 5:16-18). Pray. He hears. He speaks. He redeems. He acts. He knows what you need. He knows what's to be done, when it's to be done, how it's to be done, and He knows what He's doing. By the way, none of this is optional, nor is prayer just a good idea. It's absolutely necessary to get through the day. There are three imperatives listed in the Thessalonian passage—*rejoice*, *pray*, and *give thanks*. These are key to living a life that matters.

When God gets involved in your daily life, He moves in to orchestrate the day's events with promise and power. He comes *"riding the heavens to your help and through the skies in His majesty"* (Deuteronomy 33:26). In his classic, *The Lion, the Witch and the Wardrobe,* C.S. Lewis gave us a peek at Jesus, "the son of the great Emperor-beyond-the-Sea, *the* Lion, the great Lion, the King, the Lord of the whole wood… He'll settle the White Queen all right. It is He, not you, who will save. He's on the move…"

> Wrong will be right, when Aslan (the Lord) comes in sight,
> At the sound of his roar, sorrows will be no more,
> When he bares his teeth, winter meets its death,
> And when he shakes his mane, we shall have spring again.[131]

---

[131] C.S Lewis, *The Lion, the Witch, and the Wardrobe*, Kindle Edition, HarperCollins e-books, 2008, 48-50.

I am reminded again of how dependent I am on God's help and guidance through both the best of times and the harshest of days. Trials and tribulations drive me to my knees. Desperation takes me into the heart and throne room of God, where "wrong will be made right" and "winter meets its death."

Jonah *"prayed to the Lord his God from the stomach of a great fish"* (Jonah 2:1). He said, *"I called out of my distress to the Lord"* (v. 2), a desperate man, *"fainting away"* (v. 7), in trouble, trying to stay alive, pleading with God. It may be the best prayer he ever uttered. Nothing like a little seaweed wrapped around your head and throat (v. 5) and the smell of rotting fish for three days and nights to get your attention and help you *"remember the Lord"* (v. 7) and what He requires of you.

"Prayer," said Tim Keller, "is not a passive, calm, quiet practice." It certainly wasn't for Jonah, as he spit seawater from his mouth and nearly drowned. This was no child's prayer—"Now I lay me down to sleep, I pray the Lord my soul to keep." It was much more. Jonah was passionate, undeterred, and ready to humbly accept God's direction and decisions. He prayed with fervency for help and with humility, a prayer of surrender. It worked. The results were predictable. It was his final opportunity, his last chance to secure a life that truly mattered. Jonah mattered to God. Jonah mattered to the people of Nineveh, who stood on the precipice of divine judgment.

When I pray, I gain power with God and receive His wisdom in all matters—His goodness, His faithfulness, and His plans to make the most of daily living. This is a necessity for any man or woman. I am to keep on asking, seeking, knocking, petitioning, pleading—with tears if necessary. I must keep on storming the gates of heaven with boldness until I receive all I need for this life and the life to come (Matthew 7:7-8). I will not relent. *"Behold, the Lord's hand is not so short that it cannot save; Neither is His ear so dull that it cannot hear"* (Isaiah 59:1). He hears my cry, sees my tears, embraces my fears, understands my heart, and grasps the deepest anguish of my soul.

In his classic devotional *My Utmost For His Highest*, Oswald Chambers quoted Jesus, *"Your heavenly Father knows what things you have need of before ye ask Him"* (Matthew 6:8, KJV). Then Chambers suggested, "The point of asking is that you may get to know God better… Keep praying in order to get a perfect understanding of God Himself."[132] Mother Teresa agrees: "Prayer enlarges the heart until it is capable of containing God's gift of himself."[133]

Above all else, this was what Moses wanted—to know God personally and intimately. He prayed, *"…teach me your ways so I may know you and continue to find favor with you"* (Exodus 33:13, NIV). There was, and is, nothing more important to flesh and blood than knowing God. Nothing. The knowledge of the person of God and His presence is critical for realigning my plans with His and pushing myself toward an active, productive faith and an unwavering trust in the God who holds the whole world in His hands. Elizabeth Elliot wrote in her book *Secure in the Everlasting God*, "A prayerful heart and an obedient heart will learn, very slowly and not without sorrow, to stake everything on God Himself."[134]

---

[132] Oswald Chambers, *My Utmost for His Highest*, (Uhrichville, Ohio: Dodd, Mead & Company, 1935), March 20.
[133] Justin Portal Welby, Archbishop of Canterbury, Prayer is how we find our true identity - as individuals and as the church, retrieved from https://www.archbishopofcanterbury.org/node/478/printable/print.
[134] Elliot, Elisabeth. Secure in the Everlasting Arms: Trusting the God Who Never Leaves Your Side, (Baker Publishing Group. Kindle Edition, 2002), 30.

There are times when there is no place else to go but to God, to weep and plead before His throne of mercy and grace. Elizabeth Elliot offered this prayer by François de la Mothe Fénelon for confused, anxious pilgrims needing to hear from God.

> Lord, I know now what I ought to ask of Thee; Thou only knowest what I need: thou lovest me better than I know how to love myself. O Father! Give to Thy child that which he himself knows not how to ask. I dare not ask either for crosses or consolations; I simply present myself before Thee, I open my heart to Thee. Behold my needs which I know not myself; see and do according to thy tender mercy. Smite or heal; depress me or raise me up; I adore all Thy purposes without knowing them; I am silent; I offer myself in sacrifice; I yield myself to Thee; I would have no other desire than to accomplish Thy will. Teach me to pray. Pray thyself in me. Amen.[135]

It is critically important for me to know God, but it is just as important for me to grasp the irrefutable, precious fact that God knows me—everything about me: my pain, brokenness, doubts, worries, uncertainties, sicknesses, strengths and weaknesses, joys and sorrows, hopes and dreams. Consequently, my focus must be to know Him more and seek Him fervently if I desire to make something of my life. The better I know Him, the better my prayer life. The more honest and passionate my prayers, the greater my effectiveness in communicating with God. The more I talk with God, the deeper my inner peace and tranquility become. Knowing that God is God (Psalm 46:10, NKJV), and that there is no other, strengthens my ability to *"Be still"* in the midst of turmoil.

---

[135] Ibid, 31-32

Eventually, approaching God on my knees will lead me to trust Him more, enabling me to *"cast all (my) anxiety upon Him, because He cares for (me)"* (1 Peter 5:7). He knows me, and He is not surprised by my disappointments, worries, and fears. I can leave them behind in the capable arms of God, who is able to carry them all. Life is not too heavy for Him—He has huge shoulders. John Wesley said:

> *I have never known more than fifteen minutes of anxiety or fear. Whenever I feel fearful emotions overtaking me, I just close my eyes and thank God that He is still on the throne reigning over everything, and I take comfort in His control over the affairs of my life.*[136]

Ultimately, He has my life and yours in His hands and will give us His best. He knows what I truly want and what I truly need to build a life that works, making daily living better, fuller, and richer.

I was serving as the senior pastor of a small church in the village of Catskill, New York. I was there for nearly two decades. The years passed, and I found myself one summer on the campus of Bryan College, a conservative Christian college tucked away in the Tennessee Valley in the town of Dayton. I had never heard of Bryan before, but I was there to pursue an advanced academic degree from another institution that was using Bryan's facilities. It was a great experience. I lived in the dorm, ate cafeteria food, and met some wonderful people.

It was a typical, hot July day, and I was alone. I decided to go for a walk. As I wandered aimlessly through the campus grounds,

---

[136] Josh Mackenstein, The fearless John Wesley," *Sermon Spill-over,* June 28, 2015, retrieved from https://pastormackenstein.wordpress.com/2015/06/28/sermon-spill-over-6282015-the-fearless-john-wesley/trackback/.

my mind shot back to my seminary days, when God spoke to my heart and impressed upon me—in the library at the time—where I would serve Him in the years ahead. One day, I would minister in some capacity at a college or university. I didn't know exactly where or when, but I was certain of the path God would eventually lead me down.

I remember praying, "Lord, You know my heart. You know I would love that, but I think I need a minimum of five years of preparation in the pastorate to gain sufficient experience and knowledge to be credible when I open my mouth in the classroom." I look back now and can almost hear God's amusement with my proposal. "Yes," He might say. "You need five years, but I'm going to tack on ten more just to make sure you are fully prepared for the tasks ahead." God does know what He's doing.

That day on campus, I found myself standing alone on a hill overlooking the soccer fields. I prayed quietly. I needed to talk things over with God. I didn't ask Him for anything specific, nor did I plead my case. I didn't beg, rant, or rave. I just shared my heart honestly and openly with the Father. I prayed quietly in a whisper, "Lord, I would love someday to be at a college like Bryan, coaching soccer, preparing, and teaching young men and women to serve You and Your kingdom in the days ahead." That's all I said. Nothing more. I sighed and went on with my walk, not expecting anything to come of my short conversation with God. Little did I know that two years later, God would order my steps and bring me to Bryan to do what He had called and equipped me to do—coaching, teaching, and directing—for the next twenty-five years. God must have been listening that day on the sidelines of an empty soccer field. In the end, I got God's best. I got the desires of my heart (Psalm 37:4) and more than I could have ever imagined. If you want your life to count, talk with God.

I recently read the story of a young man who was at a Bible study where he heard a lesson about the importance of listening to God and obeying His voice. A bit skeptical, the man asked, "Does God still speak to people?" He might better have asked, "Do people still speak to God?" Either way, he was about to find out. A true story.

On the way home from church, the man thought of stopping at the store to buy a gallon of milk, though he didn't really need it. So he dismissed the notion. But the prompting in his spirit came again, only this time harder and stronger.

He said, "Okay, God. In case that is You, I will buy the milk."

He stopped, purchased the item, and resumed his journey home. That inner voice, however, would not leave him alone and urged him to turn down Seventh Street. He didn't and drove on past the intersection. The pressure to turn around and go back was instantaneous. The "voice" was clear and insistent. There was no mistaking what he had to do. God was seemingly engineering the entire event. *"My sheep listen to my voice; I know them, and they follow me"* (John 10:27).

He drove several blocks, then suddenly felt impressed to pull over to the curb. It wasn't the best of neighborhoods. Everything was closed, and most of the houses looked dark. People were apparently sleeping. But the pressure to act increased. "Go and give the milk to the people in that house." There were no other options. He had to go and deliver the milk. This was not a suggestion, but a divine appointment. Reluctantly, he went across the street and knocked on the door. God had been speaking to his heart all along.

A man came to the door wearing jeans and a T-shirt. He seemed annoyed.

"Who is it? What do you want… Well?"

"Here, I brought this for you."

The man grabbed the milk and rushed down a hallway. A baby was crying. The father sobbed, "We ran out of money and milk for the baby. We had nothing. When you knocked at the door, I had been praying and asking God to show me how to get some milk."

From the kitchen, his wife yelled out, "I asked God to send an angel with some. Are you an angel?"

The young man reached into his wallet, pulled out all the money he had, and placed it in the hands of those needy parents. He turned and walked back toward his car, weeping. Lesson learned. God still hears, God still speaks, and God still answers prayers.[137] *"I sought the LORD,"* wrote David, *"and he answered me; he delivered me from all my fears"* (Psalm 34:4, NIV). And He is still at it.

That night, the life of a young man who spoke with God mattered. What he did mattered. It mattered to a mother and father who needed help and a gallon of milk to feed their baby. A husband laid bare his heart before the throne of God, asking for help from above. A helpless mother cried to the Lord, needing divine intervention, and a young man became God's answer for a family in great need. Life works when you pray. Life matters when you talk with God… a lot.

---

[137] Steve Woods, Sr. Pastor, A young man's story – answered prayer, *Sunrise Chapel*, 2004, retrieved from http://sunrisechapel.church/a-young-mans-story-answered-prayer/.

"You Got To Get It While You Can" was a number one hit song, recorded by rock and roll icon, Janis Joplin, the last track on her 1971 posthumous album *Pearl*.[138] A song that reinforced the brevity and uncertainty of life and the need to make the most of the opportunity to make love and life count. She never made it. She was found in her Los Angeles hotel room lying dead on the floor next to her bed. She died of alcohol abuse and heroin overdose at twenty-seven years old in 1970. A life cut short in her search for fulfillment and satisfaction. Hers was the tragic loss of a woman who fully embraced the "sex, drugs, and rock and roll" philosophy of the late 1960s.[139] We never heard from Janis again…

---

[138] Janis Joplin, You got to get it while you can, (Pearl, 1971), *Songfacts*, retrieved from https://www.songfacts.com/facts/janis-joplin/get-it-while-you-can.
[139] History.com Editors, Janis Joplin dies of a heroin overdose, *History, A&E Television Networks*, November 13, 2009, retrieved from https://www.history.com/this-day-in-history/janis-joplin-dies-of-a-heroin-overdose.

CONCLUSION

In an interview with *Rolling Stone* magazine, celebrity Brad Pitt was asked about his own life and the pursuit of the American Dream. He responded,

> I know all these things are supposed to seem important to us—the car, the condo, our version of success—but if that's the case, why is the general feeling out there reflecting more impotence and isolation and desperation and loneliness? If you ask me, I say toss all this—we gotta find something else. Because all I know is that at this point in time, we are heading for a dead end, a numbing of the soul, a complete atrophy of the spiritual being. And I don't want that.
>
> I don't have those answers yet. The emphasis now is on success and personal gain. I'm sitting in it, and I'm telling you, that's not it.[140]

That never has been "it." Pitt was correct. "Toss all this." It's junk. The pursuit of fame, a little fun, and a fortune of riches is not worth the effort or the sacrifice. It never lasts anyway, and it truly never satisfies. Such a life is a dead-end street. "We gotta find something else." There is a better way to live.

Be authentic. Be real. Live under the authority of God. Know, love, and live His Word. Engage the world with the truth of the Gospel. Find and fulfill God's purpose for your life. Live in His

---

[140] Chris Heath, The unbearable bradness of being, *Rolling Stone*, October 28, 1999, retrieved from https://www.bradpittpress.com/artint_99_rollingstone.php.

presence. Get to know God more deeply. Glorify His name in attitude and action, and for heaven's sake, and for your own well-being, pray. Pray without ceasing about everything.

It does matter how you and I live. It matters how we spend our days. It matters what values and priorities we adopt and the people we see and interact with daily. It matters who my friends are, what consumes my thinking, my time, my energy, and my personal resources. It matters how we fill our days, the places we choose to go, and where it will all end when my foot hits the grave. I think I want more than transient ideals before the expiration date runs out on my daily life.

John Newton spent his early years living a life devoid of God. He lived as if God did not exist, morally blind and with a seared conscience. He was rebellious and indulged himself in every form of wickedness imaginable, including captaining his own slave trade ship—a vile man who chained men and women in irons under awful, inhuman, unimaginable conditions that cost many lives. Newton was as lost as lost can be. He admitted, "For some years I never was an hour in any company without attempting to corrupt them."[141] He summed up his life with these words: "My whole life when awake was a course of the most horrid impiety and profaneness."[142]

On March 10, 1748, Newton found himself in a raging storm on the high seas. His ship was going under; disaster seemed certain. Newton recalled that his thoughts turned to his past and the terrible things he had done. His life flashed before him, and he cried out to the very God he had offended, "Mercy! Mercy! What mercy can there be for me?"

---

[141] Seven R. Mosley, *Glimpses of God*, (Sisters, Oregon: Questar, 1990), 114.
[142] C. Knapp, John Newton, *Wholesome Words: Christian Biographies*, retrieved from https://www.wholesomewords.org/biography/bnewton10.html.

He sought the God of mercy and found Him.[143] Newton later reported that God rescued him and redeemed his miserable life—something he never got over. He remembered the love and grace of God for the rest of his days. "For on that day the Lord came from on high and delivered me out of deep waters." The man was never the same. His life became a living testimony to the glory and mercy of God. More than two hundred and fifty years later, we are still singing, *"Amazing Grace, how sweet the sound that saved a wretch like me."* Newton wrote of his own life:

> This is my testimony. This is my confession of faith. This is my hope –'It is certain that I am not what I ought to be. But, blessed be God, I am not what I once was. God has mercifully brought me up out of the deep miry clay and set my feet upon the Rock, Christ Jesus. He has saved my soul. And now it is my heart's desire to extol and honour his matchless, free, sovereign and distinguishing grace, because 'By the grace of God I am what I am.' It is my heart's great joy to ascribe my salvation entirely to the grace of God.

John Newton became a staunch abolitionist and served the church as a minister in England for some twenty years. A dramatic, stunning transformation that cannot be denied transpired in the life of a one-time sea captain who bought and sold slaves for profit. A vivid, supernatural change took place in the hardest and most callous of hearts that only God could have made happen. A one-time slave trader, who mercilessly tore families apart, brutally destroyed the lives of people, and ruined the hopes and dreams of thousands, became a lover of souls and lived a life that mattered—a life of significance, a life that made a difference in this world, in the

---

[143] Anonymous, John Newton's Conversion, *Banner of Truth*, June 1, 2001, retrieved from https://banneroftruth.org/us/resources/articles/2001/john-newtons-conversion/.

church, on the streets, in the back alleyways of cities, and on an entire continent.

You can have the same impact, the same experience, and get similar results right where God has placed you—in the backyard with your kids, in your neighborhood, at the supermarket, the local hospital, the jail, or, if need be, on a slave ship or in the jungles and remote villages of the Amazon. Wherever God takes you, follow His leading.[144] It does matter.

David Livingstone lived a life that counted. Livingstone was a Scottish missionary, linguist, scientific investigator, explorer, doctor, and abolitionist, who followed the leading of Christ in opening up Africa to the West. He died at the age of sixty. He took his last breath at four o'clock in the morning while kneeling at his bedside praying. That's how his companions found him—on his knees. Afterward, they took his heart and buried it in African soil. It was said that his heart belonged to Africa.[145] I suspect that his heart first belonged to Christ. His body, however, was returned to Britain, where it all began. He was buried at Westminster Abbey. His tombstone reads:

Missionary, Traveller, Philanthropist... For 30 years, his life was spent in an unwearied effort to evangelize the native races, to explore the undiscovered secrets, to abolish the desolating slave trade of Central Africa. With his last words, he wrote, "All I can add in my solitude is may heaven's rich blessing come down on everyone, American, English, or Turk, who will help to heal this open sore of the world.[146]"

---

[144] Ibid.
[145] Grant Oster, "His heart belongs in Africa, Part II, " *Hankering for History,* 2012, retrieved from https://hankeringforhistory.com/his-heart-belongs-in-africa-part-two/.
[146] Ross Paterson, David Livingstone - Missionary Multi-Tasker, (Blog), *Filed Partner International*, September 11, 2023, retrieved from https://www.fieldpartner.org/david-livingstone/

A clear witness to the power of God and to a man who chose well, lived well, made a difference in the world, and left behind an incredible legacy of service to God and humanity. He touched a multitude of people in his generation and beyond. He blazed new trails for the expansion of the gospel of Christ in the African continent, where he bore an abundance of fruit for the kingdom of God. Livingstone mattered. What he did mattered. Every step of the twenty-nine thousand miles he walked through the jungles of Africa in the course of his life mattered. Every turn in the road he traveled mattered. Every moment was holy. God-directed. God-approved. Every day was lived focused on what he believed God had equipped and planned for him to be and do. A British magazine paid tribute to the man and his mission with these words, "He lived and died for good…"[147]

So should it be said of every follower of Christ—me, you, all of us who would answer the call of God and journey to wherever God takes us, be it back into our home, family, marriage, even to *"Jerusalem…Judea… Samaria, and to the ends of the earth"* (Acts 1:8, NLT).

When everything is said and done, and you close your eyes for the last time on this earth, you will step through the portals of heaven and into the celestial city just over the horizon as a follower of Christ. There you shall see God, the One with the nail prints in His hands, who will give you "*an inheritance that is imperishable, undefiled, and unfading, kept in heaven for you*" (1 Peter 1:3-4, ESV). There will be joy unspeakable, unlimited mercy, and an abundance of love so marvelous, so amazing, so deep and wide, so great that the boundaries of the universe are not large enough to contain the grace of God and all His blessings extended to you and

---

[147] David B. Calhoun, David Livingstone (1813 – 1873): A profile in faith, *C.S. Lewis Institute*, September 1, 2013, retrieved from https://www.cslewisinstitute.org/resources/david-livingstone-1813-1873/.

me. You will not regret a single day spent following Christ, no matter how hard it was or how painful your days may have been. It was said of Jesus, "*For the joy set before him he endured the cross*" (Hebrews 12:2, NIV). Do no less. We have the opportunity, right now, to live like Him, to live like it matters. Remember, "You can't go back and change the beginning, but you can start where you are and change the ending." Christ lived a life that mattered. So can you. It is never too late.

My final exhortation, as you consider the principles of living a life that matters laid out in the pages of this book: Grab this life of faith in Christ by the tail and hold on for all your worth. Don't let go. It does not matter how old or young you are, whether you are rich or poor, working at McDonald's or in the corporate office of the local bank, whether you are full of life and vigor or laying in a hospital bed nearing death. Serve the King with all the passion you can muster in moving through the routine affairs of daily life, or while scaling a mountain to reach the summit of success, or in the lowest valley of tears. Oswald Chambers, in his classic devotional *My Utmost for His Highest*, wrote, "Trust entirely in God, and when He brings you to the venture, see that you take it."[148]

Let the revolution begin. Live a life that matters.

---

[148] Oswald Chambers, *My Utmost for His Highest*, (Uhrichsville, Ohio: Barbour Publishing, 1963), May 30th.

OTHER BOOKS BY SANFORD ZENSEN

- *On the Wall with Sword and Trowel* (WIPF and Stock, 2019)
- *Living Deep in a Shallow World* (WIPF and Stock, 2020)
- *The Most Important Decision You'll Ever Make* (WIPF and Stock, 2021)
- *The Divine Inquiry*, (WIPF and Stock, 2023)
- *Lord, Why? Questioning God When Life Hurts* (WIPF and Stock, 2024)

About the Author

Sanford "Sandy" Zensen is an ordained Baptist and former Christian & Missionary Alliance minister with over twenty years of pastoral ministry experience. In addition, he has served for twenty-five years as a professor of Christian studies and as a Christian college administrator. He holds two professional degrees, an MDiv and a DMin, as well as a PhD in religion and society.

Sandy is a frequent speaker at churches, men's ministries, college alumni functions, and athletic events. He was the 2014 AGS (Adult and Graduate Studies) commencement speaker at Bryan College in Tennessee and is the author of five books. He continues to serve as a member and Sunday school teacher at Stuart Heights Baptist Church, one of the largest Southern Baptist churches in Chattanooga, Tennessee.

Notes

www.ingramcontent.com/pod-product-compliance
Lightning Source LLC
Chambersburg PA
CBHW072137160426
43197CB00012B/2144